The Gleneagle

The Gleneagle

AN ILLUSTRATED HISTORY

AOIFE O'DONOGHUE & BARBARA O'DONOGHUE

The
History
Press
Ireland

For all the friends and family of
The Gleneagle who are no longer with us.

First published 2015

The History Press Ireland
50 City Quay
Dublin 2
Ireland
www.thehistorypress.ie

British Library Cataloguing in Publication Data.
A catalogue record for this book is available from the British Library.

ISBN 978 1 84588 889 3

Typesetting and origination by The History Press

Contents

Foreword

For me The Gleneagle is so much more than just a hotel. My earliest memories are of exploring and hiding in the corridors and, later, learning the trade from my parents, grandparents and many colleagues. It has always been our mission to be more – to offer more to our visitors and to do more for them too. Times have changed, our walls have grown but this ethos has and always will remain the same. Whether you are a visitor, a friend or part of our past or present team I hope you enjoy this look back in time as much as I have.

Patrick O'Donoghue,
The Gleneagle Hotel

About the Authors

AOIFE O'DONOGHUE is among the third generation of O'Donoghues to work at The Gleneagle Hotel. She is a graduate of NUI Galway having completed a BA in English and History in 2000 and an MA in Culture and Colonialism in 2002. She also holds a Higher Diploma in Journalism. Aoife is the daughter of Maurice and Margaret O'Donoghue.

BARBARA O'DONOGHUE is a PhD student in the School of History at University College Cork. She completed a BA in 2008 after which she specialised in History, receiving first-class honours for her MA in Historical Research. She recently completed her doctoral thesis on US Foreign Policy in Southeast Asia during the 1970s. Barbara is a granddaughter of the late Paddy and Sheila O'Donoghue.

Acknowledgements

We would like to thank, in particular, the photographers who have documented the hotel's history through their work and who have contributed to this book. A busy business means there is often little time to take notes and so the wealth of pictures featured here are an invaluable piece of our history. Thank you Valerie O'Sullivan, Don MacMonagle, Eamonn Keogh, Michelle Cooper-Galvin, Kevin Coleman, Nerijus Karmilcovas and Andrew Bradley. Similarly the archives of *The Kerryman* and *The Kingdom* newspapers at Kerry County Library and Killarney Library were a great source of information and provided some interesting perspectives. Thank you to the staff of both libraries, in particular Michael Lynch, for your patience and help. For the archivists in the O'Donoghue family, thank you for preserving and safeguarding the many photos, newspaper clippings and priceless recollections. Thank you Dr William Sheehan for your guidance and support. Thanks also to Ronan Colgan and Beth Amphlett at The History Press Ireland for bringing this project to life.

Introduction

The walls of The Gleneagle Hotel don't talk: they sing. The following pages recount many of their tunes but there is simply not enough space or pictures for the entire anthology. These walls have witnessed millions of memorable moments, first glances, first dances and many first romances. First giggles, last laughs, life and love celebrated, these memories are enshrined forever within the walls of this wonderful hotel. From modest beginnings as a small country house, The Gleneagle has flourished into one of Ireland's largest and best-known holiday destinations. Its story is one of expansion and growth, but also of challenges and risks.

The Gleneagle was originally known as Flesk House. It was a Georgian house built in the 1830s. It sat on four acres and had a cobbled courtyard and an orchard. In 1957, the house and grounds were purchased by Paddy and Sheila O'Donoghue for £5,000. Originally from the neighbouring parish of Glenflesk, Paddy O'Donoghue served as an apprentice chemist to Mr Hartnett in Killarney's Henn Street (now Plunkett Street) before going on to UCD for his MPSI course. After he qualified, Paddy returned to Killarney to P.D. Foley's chemist shop, which he bought in 1926. In 1936, he married Sheila O'Donoghue of Foley's Bar in New Street in Killarney. In 1957 Paddy and Sheila, along with their seven children, moved from their family home above Paddy's chemist in Main Street to Flesk House on Muckross Road. While the house afforded more space in which to raise their children, the couple also recognised the property's commercial potential and within months welcomed their first paying guests.

Paddy decided that Flesk House was not a marketable name for a hotel. Keen to put his own stamp on the building, he combined the name of his native townland of Glenflesk with the local knowledge that the Muckross area had been a rare breeding ground for eagles, and on 11 October 1957 The Gleneagle was registered as a licensed hotel. The O'Donoghues' entrepreneurial spirit came to the fore again in 1959, when they built a dancehall adjacent to the hotel. Their eldest son Maurice, who was studying Pharmacy in Dublin at the time, drove home three to four nights a week to run dances. A young and enthusiastic Maurice prioritised 'quality above all' and consistently booked the very best in top bands and shows, filling a huge gap in the night life of Killarney, and attracting punters from throughout Kerry and the adjoining counties.

While those attending the dances were Irish, the guests of the hotel in the early years hailed predominately from Britain and the US, a pattern reflected throughout Killarney. The O'Donoghues recognised the domestic tourist market was largely untapped and underdeveloped and so set about enticing Ireland's own to holiday in the burgeoning tourist town.

The strategy was not to rely simply on Killarney's natural beauty to attract visitors but to offer activities, entertainment and value for money as well. And so, the O'Donoghues set about developing The Gleneagle into an all-inclusive holiday destination. Squash courts, pitch and putt courses, tennis courts and a leisure centre were gradually added, as were guestrooms of varying styles and sizes. All sorts of holiday packages were introduced and marketed, from the Showtime Express to ballroom dancing breaks.

Entertainment too played its part and following on from the success of the showband era, The Gleneagle Summer Cabaret was introduced in 1965. Visitors holidaying all over Kerry flocked to the hotel's ballroom and the cabaret became an intrinsic part of summer in Killarney. Entertainment wasn't just limited to the summer months; in fact, by the mid-1990s The Gleneagle Hotel hosted live shows every single night of the year. Then, at the turn of the millennium, Maurice and Margaret O'Donoghue opened Ireland's National Events Centre (INEC). This state-of-the-art facility meant that top-selling international artists and bands could perform in Killarney for the very first time. Today, The Gleneagle Hotel is considered one of Ireland's leading entertainment venues and hosts a wide range of events all-year-round.

The versatility of the INEC allows it not only to host live shows and concerts, but also to be transformed into a world-class conference venue. Constantly identifying and courting new ideas and markets, Killarney Convention Centre was launched to promote The Gleneagle Hotel, the INEC and all its facilities to the corporate world. Today The Gleneagle Hotel is not only a leisure and entertainment destination, it is also a place of business where politicians, organisations and blue-chip companies gather to get work done.

Behind all the changes, developments, trials and triumphs of The Gleneagle Hotel, lies the passion and dedication of the team of staff. 'Our people are our best asset', Maurice O'Donoghue told *The Examiner* in 1998. Today, the hotel employs around 300. Their devotion and passion is palpable, and their can-do attitude is applauded by the hotel's visitors every day. The Gleneagle Hotel is now under the guardianship of the third generation of O'Donoghues: Maurice and Margaret's son Patrick and his wife Eileen. Sixty years and three generations on, the O'Donoghues and their team continue to improve, expand and develop their family business.

CHAPTER ONE

Hotel History and Development

From modest beginnings as a small country house hotel, first opened in 1957, The Gleneagle has flourished into one of Ireland's largest and most popular hotels. The original Georgian walls still stand in the heart of the hotel, and the entrepreneurial spirit that first inspired a young Killarney family to turn their home into a business endures to this day.

The O'Donoghue children playing outside Flesk House in 1957. Flesk House was purchased by Paddy and Sheila O'Donoghue in 1957 as a family home but within months they had welcomed their first paying guests. 'The Lake Hotel was overbooked one night and the Huggard family asked if we could give them rooms and that's how it started,' Sheila explained to the *Irish Independent* ('Sheila Stands Up to be Counted for a 16th Time,' *Irish Independent*, 9 April 2011).

The Gleneagle Hotel was originally known as Flesk House. It was an eight-bedroom Georgian building constructed in the 1830s as a private home for one of the Herberts of Cahernane. It later became the stately home of Lord Headley. The house was first opened as a hotel by Eustace McMorough-Bernard, a member of a famous Killarney family and later passed into the hands of Mr William Gilmore who also ran a thriving hotel. The house then reverted to the role of a private residence when bought by Archie Graham.

Flesk House was purchased by Paddy and Sheila O'Donoghue in 1957 for the princely sum of £5,000. The two-storey building sat on four acres and had a cobbled courtyard and an orchard. Initially the house afforded more space in which to raise their seven children, but the couple also recognised the property's commercial potential and within months welcomed their first paying guests. An independent-minded man and an original thinker, Paddy O'Donoghue decided that Flesk House was not a marketable name for a hotel. He combined the name of his native townland of Glenflesk with the local knowledge that the Muckross area had been a rare breeding ground for eagles and on 11 October 1957 The Gleneagle was registered as a licensed hotel.

At the time of purchase by the O'Donoghues, Flesk House was around 120 years old. It had eight large bedrooms and was sited on four acres of ground. In the first year, six additional bedrooms were added, followed by twelve more bedrooms and the ballroom the following year.

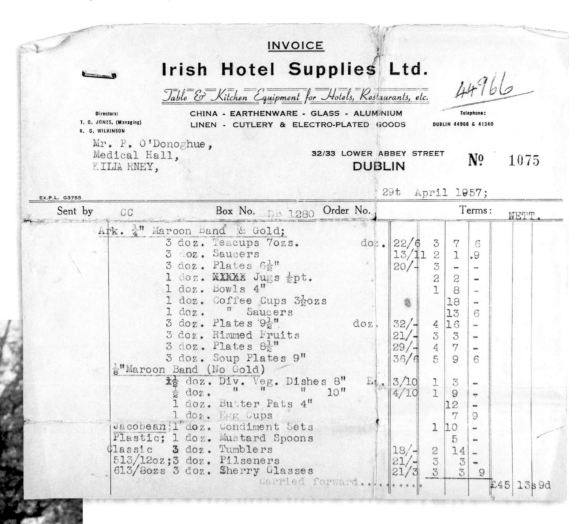

INVOICE

Irish Hotel Supplies Ltd.

Table & Kitchen Equipment for Hotels, Restaurants, etc.

44966

CHINA - EARTHENWARE - GLASS - ALUMINIUM
LINEN - CUTLERY & ELECTRO-PLATED GOODS

Directors:
T. G. JONES, (Managing)
R. G. WILKINSON

Telephone:
DUBLIN 44966 & 41340

Mr. P. O'Donoghue,
Medical Hall,
KILLARNEY,

32/33 LOWER ABBEY STREET
DUBLIN

N⁰ 1075

Ex.P.L. G3755

29t April 1957;

Sent by	Box No.	Order No.		Terms:
CC	DB 1280			NETT.

Ark. ¼" Maroon Band & Gold;							
3 doz. Teacups 7ozs.	doz.	22/6	3	7	6		
3 doz. Saucers		13/11	2	1	.9		
3 doz. Plates 6½"		20/-	3	-	-		
1 doz. Milk Jugs ½pt.			2	2	-		
1 doz. Bowls 4"			1	8	-		
1 doz. Coffee Cups 3½ozs				18	-		
1 doz. " Saucers				13	6		
3 doz. Plates 9½"	doz.	32/-	4	16	-		
3 doz. Rimmed Fruits		21/-	3	3	-		
3 doz. Plates 8½"		29/-	4	7	-		
3 doz. Soup Plates 9"		36/6	5	9	6		
⅛"Maroon Band (No Gold)							
1½ doz. Div. Veg. Dishes 8"	Ea.	3/10	1	3	-		
½ doz. " " " 10"		4/10	1	9	-		
1 doz. Butter Pats 4"				12	-		
1 doz. Egg Cups				7	9		
Jacobean;1 doz. Condiment Sets			1	10	-		
Plastic; 1 doz. Mustard Spoons				5	-		
Classic 3 doz. Tumblers		18/-	2	14	-		
513/12oz;3 doz. Pilseners		21/-	3	3	-		
613/8ozs 3 doz. Sherry Glasses		21/3	3	3	9		
Carried forward..........						£45	13s 9d

Invoice to The Gleneagle
Hotel from Irish Hotel
Supplies Ltd, 29 April 1957.

The Gleneagle Hotel welcomed its first
guests in the summer of 1957.

Date of Arrival	Name	Address	In Full	Nationality	Room No.	Date of Departure
June 15, 1957	Mary O'Hare	2421 Dickey Place	Houston 19, Texas	U.S.A	22	June 17
June 15, 1957	Margaret Hughes	2520 Pelham Drive	Houston 19, Texas	U.S.A	18	June 17
15/6/9		Poplands Texas	London	British	20	—
15/6/57	Elizabeth H. Graham	184 Oak Hill Ave.	Pawtucket, R.I.	American	18	June 17
10/6/57	Constance M. Corr	12 Cedar Ave.	Westfield. Mass.	U.S.A	8	June 17
15/6/57	Jean Marie Kraff	256 Bay View Road	Rochester 9. New York	American	22	June 17
6/14/57	Barbara G. Burke	63 Elle St.	Littlefield, Mass	U.S.A	8	June 16th
6-15-57	Lois Hansen	213 do. 12th Avenue	Yakima, Washington	U.S.A.	14	June 16th
6-15-57	Donna Renoward	Mt. Con Mine Residence	Butte, Montana U.S.A.	U.S.A	16	June 16th
6-15-57	Donna Fatty	Box 141	Bismarck North Dakota U.S.A	American	15	June 16th
6-15-57	Janet Jill	341 NE Floral Place	Portland, Oregon	American	12	June 15th
6-15-57	Kathleen Quinn	7 Kentisle Lane	San Rafael, Calif.	U.S.A	14	June 16th
6-15-57	Patricia Rocke	219 S. 24th Ave.	Yakima, Washington	American	12	June 16
6-16-57	Mary Ann Onorato	36 Crane Drive	San Anselmo, Calif.	U.S.A.	15	June 16th
July 15, 1957	Mr & Mrs Ryan	Dublin		Irish	21	
July 15	John Renkeroll			"		
"	Patrick White			"		
"	Noelle White			"		
"	Alex & Reinhardt			"		
"	Eileen Frant	Tralee		"	10	
"	James Walsh	Tralee		"	11	
"	James Walsh	Tralee				

Hotel register, 15 June 1957.

The Gleneagle Hotel, 1961. The ballroom, seen to the right of the photo, was added in 1959. A new extension was added in 1961, including a balcony designed by Tralee architect Patrick O'Sullivan and three large dome windows that overlooked the lawns of the hotel. The mineral bar was replaced by a cafeteria and bar and the room was completely soundproofed to prevent noise from reaching the bedrooms above. The ballroom was officially opened in July 1961 and that summer the hotel began a free bus service for patrons of the dances using two Volkswagen micro-buses in red and white. (© Harry MacMonagle, macmonagle.com)

Advertisement,
Irish Independent, 7 July 1959.

GlenEagle Hotel, *Killarney*

KILLARNEY'S NEWEST
AND
MOST MODERN HOTEL

Standing on 4 acres of verdant terraced lawns. Enchanting view from every bedroom. Central Heating. Spacious, soundproof ballroom with sprung maple floor.

Weddings, Socials and Parties Specially Catered For. Fully Licensed.

TELEPHONE: KILLARNEY 100

The Dining Room, added
to the hotel in 1960. (© Harry
MacMonagle, macmonagle.com)

A front view of Killarney's expanding GlenEagle Hotel

KILLARNEY'S GLENEAGLE HOTEL KEEPS GROWING

By PATRICK W. SMYTH

THIS is the story of one man's success and of a united family's triumph. It is the Twentieth Century fairytale of the boy who set out to make his fortune, and found that Killarney's streets were paved with gold. The hero of this story had no fortune left to him other than the gifts of an acute business brain, the capacity for hard work and a driving ambition to succeed. With these gifts at his command the man from Glenflesk needed no magic wand to make his impact on the life of Killarney.

When he arrived as an apprentice chemist in Killarney many more years ago than he cares to remember, young Paddy O'Donoghue was concerned with only one thing—to make his way in the world. He never dreamed that he would find himself going into the hotel business in the years that lay ahead. His future seemed mapped out for him. But Fate must have reckoned without the ambition of Paddy O'Donoghue.

fresh fields

Ambition it was that drove him on until he set up business in his own chemist shop on Main Street, Killarney. Business gradually improved thanks to Paddy's hard work and genial manner behind the counter. The shop improved. Soon, it absorbed a public house next door, which is now part of the extensive premises. Before long, O'Donoghue's was one of the finest chemist shops in Ireland.

But Paddy O'Donoghue still looked for fresh fields to conquer. The lad who fought through the hell of the Black and Tan War and the Civil War Period in Ireland was not the one to rest his spirit on the laurels of relatively easy conquest. He acquired another premises in Killarney, found them unsuited to his purposes, discarded them. He felt that his shop in Main Street could hardly be improved further, and he looked around for something bigger to occupy his ambition.

When he heard that the premises now known as the Glen Eagle Hotel, Killarney, was up for sale, he decided that here was the opportunity he had been waiting for.

Paddy didn't let any grass grow under his feet. He bought the premises and all effects in it in one evening. In cold fact, the "deal" for the hotel was really clinched in a fifteen-minute conversation. And the time of Paddy O'Donoghue's greatest achievement was at hand.

ample space

He found that his property covered four acres of ground bordering on two roads, one leading to Flesk Castle and the other to Kenmare, Muckross and Dinis, the heart of Killarney's scenic delights. The property was situated within easy reach of Killarney.

The premises consisted of a large private house (built 120 years ago) with eight huge bedrooms. There was ample space surrounding the house, the site for the extensive free car parks of today's hotel.

The first year, under Mr. O'Donoghue's dynamic management, six new bedrooms were added. The next year twelve new bedrooms and the ballroom were built.

Last summer a new dining-room was built and last winter a new sun lounge at the entrance to the hotel—quite a feature this!

This year, an extension to the existing ballroom was added. When I called to the GlenEagle this week I found the mineral bar erected so carefully two years ago being wrecked with a hammer. It has given way to a new cafeteria and bar, built on a level with the new, luxurious balcony that now overlooks the dancing floor. At the cafeteria the dancers may buy coffee, tea, snacks, minerals, cigarettes and the like.

Guests who require more substantial meals can obtain them in the dining hall of the hotel proper. Special waitresses will be in attendance at the cafeteria.

Overlooking the sprung maple dancefloor is a very extensive new balcony where dancers "sitting it out" can watch the others on the floor or take light refreshments at the tables provided. Access to the balcony is gained by means of two sets of wide stairs.

The new balcony can seat hundreds of patrons. At the rear of the balcony are three enormous windows overlooking the lawns of GlenEagle Hotel.

The architect was Mr. Patrick O'Sullivan of Tralee. The contractors for the original ballroom were John Sisk and Son, Cork, and the contractors for the extensions to the ballroom this year O'Brien and Sons, Killarney.

striking feature

A striking feature of the ballroom is the use of Unitone acoustical tiles on the ceiling. These very modern tiles, in addition to their acoustical properties, provide thermal insulation. Of particular interest to

intending guests of the hotel is the fact that not a sound from the ballroom can penetrate the floor to the twelve luxurious new bedrooms built immediately above the ballroom.

Architect O'Sullivan was responsible for the colour scheme in the ballroom. The ceiling has a striking but discreet pattern in pastel grey and pink. The walls are in light grey and pink, and the general effect is of streamlined modernity.

The need for the thermal insulation in the ceiling is apparent when it is considered that the floor above the ballroom is heated to provide warmth in the bedrooms. By using tiles which provide insulation, the heat is made to rise through the bedroom floors rather than go down into the ballroom.

Above the ballroom is a completely new wing, built within the last two years. Numerous windows provide ample light in the generously wide corridors, carpeted in deep grey and having a pale lilac ceiling and white or cream walls.

built-in fittings

All the larger fittings in those new rooms are built-in. A feature of all rooms is the very attractive rich oak wall panelling, the built-in lighting units, the very ample mirrors and the contemporary style furniture. Carpets have bright floral patterns on a cream background. The total effect is one of brightness and comfort. It is not unlikely, I believe, that the GlenEagle Hotel may soon be re-graded.

Bathrooms and toilets in the new wing are ultra modern. The walls and fittings are white and the brilliant blue and yellow tiles on the floors add a touch of brightness.

Nothing has been overlooked in this very progressive hotel. Entrance to the GlenEagle is gained through a new, luxurious sun lounge. The exterior is very modern in appearance, employing a huge area of glass and in-

corporating very large windows. A white globe provides illumination above the entrance. At both ends of the sun lounge two electric "lanterns," in wrought iron, lend distinction to the clean frontage.

The floor of the sun lounge is tiled in attractive and brightly coloured tiles of very pleasing design. Wickerwork lounge chairs suggest ease and comfort immediately on entering the GlenEagle Hotel, thus making an extremely good first impression.

Restful armchairs and settees greet the visitor in the foyer of the hotel, where the walls are painted in a pleasing lilac shade and the lush grey carpet has attractive geometrical patterns traced on it. The Residents' Lounge has a deep pile carpet in a rich wine red with floral patterns. The bar is modern and ample, built for ease and comfort.

dome windows

Most striking feature of the new dining-room is the three huge dome windows which provide sufficient light at all times of the year. The material for the domes was specially imported. From the huge bay window at the front of the dining hall one can obtain a grand view of Mangerton and the famous Lakes.

The walls are painted in pastel pink. The ceiling is white. The floor is equipped with thermostatically controlled floor heating, a relatively new idea, that, in Irish hotels.

The ballroom, ably managed by Mr. O'Donoghue's son Maurice (22), is one of the most successful features of this fine hotel. The policy of this young ballroom manager has been the policy of the hotel: "Quality above all." He has endeavoured to attract and hold patronage by providing the very best in top-line bands and entertainment stars, both from Ireland and from England.

endless list

To name but a few of the more familiar bands, the Glen Eagle has presented for your dancing pleasure to date: The Clipper Carlton, the Royal Showband, the Dixielanders, Kevin Flynn, the Skyrockets, Michael O'Callaghan, the Swingtime Aces, the Blue Aces, Kevin Woods, Johnny Flynn, Earl Gill and the Savoy Swing Sevens, Chris Lamb -

The list seems endless, and from a quick glance at it, it's easy for any dancing fan to understand the great success of this energetic and enthusiastic young ballroom manager.

From cross-channel names to appear at the GlenEagle I pick just a few: Michael Holliday, Anne Shelton, Rickie Valance and the Clyde Valley Stompers. Billy Williams of Killarney is the semi-resident danceband.

opening July 6

For the opening of the new ballroom on July's young Maurice O'Donoghue has engaged the existing Mighty Rhythm Boys from Buncrana, one of the liveliest combinations ever to come out of the Great North Country. When these boys come down south at the border I dare say there won't be a still foot in the whole of the GlenEagle Ballroom—and that's saying something when I understand that the new ballroom will be able to accommodate about 1,000 patrons.

Incidentally, it's of interest to note that while the new extension to the ballroom was being built the old ballroom never

(Continued on page 5)

The Kerryman, Saturday, July 1, 1961 5

The only Ballroom with a free Bus Service

from page 4

closed, quite a tribute to contractor Charles O'Brien of Killarney.

The GlenEagle does a big business with wedding parties, which have come from such areas as Castleisland, Buttevant, Dublin, Ardfert, Ballybunion, Kilorglin, Tralee, Sneem, Kenmare and Dingle. Wedding guests have the faciliity of the ballroom and the run of the hotel.

in good hands

Maurice O'Donoghue, manager of the ballroom, claims that the GlenEagle ballroom is the only one in the South of Ireland with its own free bus service. This year the hotel has two new Volkswagen micro-buses in gleaming red and white. Both buses have brilliant flashing signs on top. Their distinctive markings make them easily recognisable in the welter of traffic that flows ceaselessly through Killarney these days.

Dancers intending to patronise the GlenEagle ballroom may avail of the free bus service. On wet nights it is particularly welcome. Patrons who telephone the hotel will be collected and transported to the ballroom free of charge.

For motorists the ample space around the hotel provides free parking facilities, an important matter this at a time when such accommodation is at a premium everywhere.

Three car park attendants in white uniforms and peaked caps attend the car parks for all dancers, so you can rest assured that your old jalopy or Rolls will be in the best of hands!

Mr. and Mrs. O'Donoghue, who own the GlenEagle, have seven of a family: Maurice (22), Eileen (20), Brid, Maura (17), Aideen (15), Padraig (12) and little Anna Maria (9).

the staff

Their staff are: Freddie Healy, porter, who has been with the GlenEagle since it opened about five years ago; chef Jimmy Sugrue of Milltown; Miss Mary Anne Gleeson, cook, Killarney; Nora Luney, Killarney; Helen Casey, Kilmallock; Mary O'Boyle, Killarney (waitresses); waiters Denis Carey, Dermot Carey (both Kilsarvan) and Jimmy Healy of Killarney; Maureen O'Leary, Scartaglin, cook; Maura McGough and Brid Tangney of Killarney.

Redheaded Maura O'Donoghue who was educated at the local Mercy Loreto Convent, is the musician of the family, being an accomplished pianist. She helps generally in the hotel.

Maurice (22) was educated at the Presentation Monastery, Killarney, and Blackrock College, Dublin. He works at his father's chemist shop in Main Street and devotes most of his spare time to the GlenEagle Hotel.

Eileen was educated at the Loreto and Mercy Convents. She underwent a two years' course at Shannon Airport School; one year's training in a German hotel and is now in a Swiss hotel. A fluent German speaker, Eileen must now be knuckling down to learning French in Switzerland.

Brid helps in the administrative side of the hotel's affairs. Educated at the Mercy Convent, Killarney, Loreto Convent, Stephen's Green, Dublin and at the Pharmaceutical College, Shrewsbury Road, Dublin, she is extremely valuable at the GlenEagle.

Aideen, Padraig and Anna Maria are still at school.

What about Mr. Patrick O'Donohue, the man who started the whole thing rolling in the first place?

a memento

Paddy O'Donoghue was a pioneer of the Killarney Races, of which he was a director for seven years. He retired his directorship owing to pressure of business. He also was a director of Killarney Development Company, but had to leave this behind too, to devote more time to his private interests.

When the Killarney Estate was offered for sale he offered a cheque for £500 to the Development Company to help purchase the estate for the town. The cheque was returned later but he still holds it as a memento of the time when a group of Americans answered the question in the familiar song: "How can you buy Killarney?"

The diningroom at the GlenEagle Hotel.

The buses which convey patrons free of charge to dances at the GlenEagle Hotel Ballroom. Drivers are Paddy O'Connor (right) and Con O'Keeffe.
(Kerryman Photo)

He attributes his great success in business, typically, to hard work. "In my time I often worked fifteen hours a day, from nine in the morning until 11 at night," said Mr. O'Donoghue.

Paddy O'Donoghue had no huge inheritance to help him when he was starting up in business so many years ago. "I am a working man. Neither myself nor any member of my family has ever been afraid of hard work."

swimming pool?

To-day, Paddy O'Donoghue still wends the grounds of the GlenEagle Hotel himself. Not long ago he took great satisfaction in successfully running the 1½ acres of the Kenmare Gardens which he bought in 1941. During the war his great delight was to work in the gardens; his great regret was that due to rising costs he was forced to sell it.

The extensions that have just been completed will make the GlenEagle Hotel one of the finest in Heaven's Reflex. But, true to the O'Donoghue tradition, further extension work is planned for next year. The ballroom, even though it can now accommodate 1,000 dancers on the floor and

hundreds more in the balconies, will be expanded even further.

Maurice O'Donoghue has dreams of a swimming pool at the hotel. For many that would remain a dream but knowing the O'Donoghue spirit of ambition I have little doubt that the next

few years will see it become a reality.

When in Killarney why not pay a visit to the GlenEagle? The personal service that is a speciality there is bound to impress you.

MR. C. COURTNEY IS NEW CHAIRMAN OF KILLARNEY U.D.C.

AFTER fourteen years Killarney Urban Council has a new chairman. At the annual meeting Mr. Henry J. Downing, who held the office for that period, refused to go forward and Mr. C. Courtney was unanimously elected.

WITHDREW

Mr. Downing was proposed by Mr. D. J. O'Shea but refused to accept the proposition and explained to the Council members that for personal reasons he did not wish to seek re-election.

"After one 14 years ago I again propose you," said Mr. O'Shea.

"Thank you very much," said Mr. Downing, "but I have definitely decided not to go forward. I fully appreciate you asking me to reconsider my decision but I am not prepared to do it."

Mr. M. Moynihan then proposed the outgoing vice-chairman, Mr. C. MacSweeney for the chair and Mr. D. J. O'Shea seconded.

LONGEST SERVICE

Mr. Hussey proposed Mr. C. Courtney and said that Mr. Courtney had the longest service in the Council. He had served 27 years as a councillor "and it is his duty to take the chair."

Mr. D. Doona seconded and endorsed what was said by Mr. Hussey.

Messrs. Moynihan and O'Shea said they would withdraw their proposition and they would not proposed Mr. MacSweeney had they known that Mr. Courtney would accept the office.

He refused to accept it on numerous occasions previously, they said.

WITHDREW

Mr. MacSweeney said he would withdraw his name and Mr. Courtney was then declared unanimously elected.

Mr. Courtney thanked the members and said he would do his best to meet the wishes of the Council during his period of office.

He paid a tribute to Mr. Downing who had ruled over the Council for such a long period in a fair and equitable manner.

The best tribute he could pay him was to express the hope that he would manage the affairs of the Council in as good a manner as Mr. Downing had.

VICE-CHAIRMAN

When Mr. Moynihan proposed Mr. C. MacSweeney, the outgoing vice-chairman for that position, Mr. MacSweeney said he would withdraw his name and proposed Mr. T. P. Clifford for the office.

Mr. H. J. Downing seconded and Mr. Clifford was declared elected unanimously.

Mr. Clifford thanked the members for his election.

Date of Arrival	Name	Address	In Full	Nationality	Room No.	Date of Departure
	Mrs Marshall & Quinn	55 Sir Johns Park	Belfast N.I.	Irish	32	
	Mr & Mrs Humphreys	16, The College, St Sutton	Wind. Dublin	Bristol	25	
	Mr & Mrs E Watts	188 Whitworth Rd	Lavender Hill's Roney	British	21	
		24 Lansdm Rd	West Hill Lang	"	8	
7. 8. 60	Mr Alex Olsen & Party	1134 Eb 17th East	Salt Lake City, Utah, USA	American	37 7 28	
"	Mr P L R Raff	73 Durland Ave	Russell, Staffs.	British	30. 31.	
"	J Webb	155 Foffries Rd		Irish	15 716	
7/8/60	Miss C L Lawrence	11 Chichester Pk	Belfast	Irish	21	
7 8 60	C Smith	29 Winters Rd	London	British	26	
	W Kennedy	17 Blofield Gdns	London	Irish	24	
7/8 60	Mr & Mrs P S Rogers	68 Kilmore Rd	London	British	8	
7/8/60	Mr & Mrs H B Eastwood	Denbath Box	Cookstown Co Tyrone	Irish	12	
	Mr W Kee & Angela		Llangear Co Derry	Irish	14	
7/8/60	Mr & Mrs Mitchell	Ardwallen	Camberslang		52	
8/8/60	Jack Kearney	Drumpark Coleen		Irish	33	
August 7	W Berry	Hurten dr Bournemouth		British	10	
	Mr & Mrs H W Prince	Tamworth	New Hampshire	American	24	
	J O'Reilly	D 20,9,43 A			29	
	W Harris, Ann-Mees	11 Anget Cru Miles Avenue	England	Bristol		
	J Hennessy	3 New Bremoalt Par.	Frome			
	Mr & Mrs C B Losby	The Lodge, Aster Flamville	Mr Hinckley Leics.	British		
8/8/60	R Barry (& Mrs)	Limerick	2 Careys Rd	Irish	16	9 AM 1/8/60

Hotel register, August 1960.

Date of Arrival	Name	Address	In Full	Nationality	Room No.	Date of Departure
22/5/61	E J Musgrave	10. Fispral Lane,	London, N.4 3	British		
22/5/61	J Foster	% Australia House	the Strand London	Australian		
	W Tagor	% Canada House,	London	Canadian	8	
23/5/.	L. Mr McCabe	23 Glasgow Rd. Paisley, Scotland		British		
23/5/61	Ann Downey	South Square	Macroom, Co. Cork			
23/5/61	Nan Kelleher	Mount Cross Clonbroka				
23/5/61	Breda Dennehy	Carrigamive Macroom	Co Cork			
23/5/61	Mary Kelleher	Main Street,	Macroom, Co Cork Antrim			
23/5/61	Gabrielle Downey	South Square	Macroom Co Cork Antrim			
23/5/61	Gabrielle Breeden	Mazzy Town	Macroom Co Cork Antrim			
23/5/61	Margaret J Kirby	100 Pierce St	Hyde Park Mass USA	American		
23/5/61	Katherine Hodgins	100 Pierce St	U. S. A			
24/5/61	Mr & Mrs T H McCurdy	14 Kenhouse Sq Rathmns Dublin				
24/5/61	Mr & Mrs A H Winnie	280 Beeralane	Mol, Belgium	U.S.A.		
25/5/61	Mr & Mrs J Hilal	18 Clarendon Rd	Eccles Manchester	British		
	Mr & Mrs M Hurlbatch	9 Ventesta Avenue	Pendleton Salford 6	—		
24/5/61	Mr & Mrs R Rice	4 Langley Drive	Kingley NW9	"		
	John McAdam	11 Peckforge Newcastle		"		
	Mr & Mrs A Smith	Prome Canada		"		
	Mr & Mrs John McBean	Romera Donegal		Irish	8	24
27. 5.61	Mr & Mrs Jewchins	103 Burgh Riverip	Indea	British	31	1

Hotel register, May 1961.

In 1962 a third floor, comprising of
ten additional bedrooms, was added.

(© Harry MacMonagle, macmonagle.com)

In the following two years the hotel underwent further renovations. In 1963 a major extension to the ballroom
gave patrons 5,500sq ft of dancing space. 'You have to keep on modernising your hotel to keep up with the
times. It is no good being timid about it and thinking that it would be rash to alter anything,' Paddy O'Donoghue
commented in *The Kerryman*, 13 April 1963. (© Harry MacMonagle, macmonagle.com)

The Kerryman, Saturday, April 13, 1963.

GLENEAGLE SPREADS ITS WINGS

A panoramic view of Killarney's growing GlenEagle Hotel. On the right is the Ballroom which has been extended for the comfort of dancing patrons, and which now has its own entrance.
(Kerryman)

KILLARNEY BALLROOM gets more DANCING space,
LUXURY BEDROOMS are added to HOTEL

By
MARGARET REGAN

IT was raining . . . soft, fine misty . . . and although the thought occurred to me that when Mother Nature created Killarney she planned for the sun to shine constantly in order to show off this little bit of heaven to its best advantage, the rain did not seem to take from Killarney that day, but only served to enhance the breath-taking scenery around me.

It was still raining when, from beneath the protective shade of my umbrella, the GlenEagle Hotel came into view and despite the wetness of the day, I paused to admire the exterior of the building with its fine clean lines and panorama windows.

Despite the weather the hotel gave an impression of warmth and sunshine and I wandered inside to have a look at its newly extended ballroom and to have a stroll through the hotel to see the luxury bedrooms which also have been added.

Painters were perched precariously on ladders giving the interior walls a face-lift for the coming season. The rich, luxurious carpets in the reception lounge were concealed with protective coverings as a guard against paint splashes and while I waited to meet Mrs. Sheila O'Donoghue, two poodles, their noses pressed against the glass door of the residents' lounge, kept a watchful eye on the 'visitor.'

I always have the feeling that a hotel in the "off-season" has an air of waiting. As though everything and everyone in it are waiting for the season's visitors to flock in. Then the pace is fast and furious. But I learned at the GlenEagle that the tempo they during the Winter months has been pretty breath-taking. Contractors, designers, interior decorators, carpenters and what have you, have all been swarming about the hotel working on various projects which the proprietor, Mr. Patrick J. O'Donoghue, is having carried out.

keeps growing

The GlenEagle is a hotel which keeps on growing. In recent times it has been extended upwards and outwards and still Mr. O'Donoghue plans more extensions and alterations. "You have to keep on modernising your hotel to keep up with the times. It's no good being timid about it and thinking that it would be rash to alter anything," commented Mr. O'Donoghue.

His wife, Mrs. O'Donoghue, had a warm smile and a handshake for me on my arrival and then introduced me to her son, Maurice, manager of the Ballroom, who took me along to meet his father and to see Killarney's ballroom of the future.

Twenty-four years old Maurice is pretty enthusiastic about the new ballroom, which has been extended outwards by some 50 feet to give patrons some five thousand five hundred square feet of dancing space.

Work began last September and although when I called the interior decorations were not completed, I thought the ballroom one of the most spacious and colourful that I have seen.

A feature of the building is the feeling of space which one gets and the absolute luxury of the ballroom.

unique idea

Leaving the Canadian maple wood dance floor, patrons can relax on the comfortable padded seating which runs around the

walls and is one step off the dance floor. This has been covered in attractive rust red with splashes of black and yellow through it and is backed by gleaming rose red coloured mahogany.

In the centre of the floor two huge pillars of stone support the ceiling where last year, the hall ended.

"When they were taking away the wall we got tree trunks from the forest to support it. They looked so beautiful that we decided to have something similar to tree trunks and that is how these pillars came to be here," explained Mr. O'Donoghue, while Maurice nodded agreement. "We are waiting now for artists to come from Dublin to plan the colour scheme and also to design these pillars to fit in with our scheme," he added.

A unique idea I thought and one which is sure to add further charm to an already beautiful ballroom. Mr. O'Donoghue explained, however, that a great deal of thought was being given to the 'tree trunks' in order that they will not scratch or catch clothing and stockings worn by the ladies.

new entrance

"That would never do," he said laughingly as he pointed out special features of the elevated stage. This, I was informed has been extended more than seventeen feet and is fronted by scrolls of wrought iron braiding to prevent dancers from sitting on the edge of the stage.

"That would take from the appearance of the stage," Mr. O'Donoghue pointed out, as I admired the silver moonlight grey curtains which run along the back. More than twelve interchangeable ceiling lights have also been fitted.

In direct contrast to the muted pastel shades of the walls and curtains, are the panels of multicoloured stone-work at each side of the stage and at various vantage points around the ballroom. The stone-work blends in with the

more modern decorations and paintwork and lends a freshness to the overall appearance of the hall.

Since the alterations the ballroom now has its own entrance.

The spacious car park attached to the GlenEagle Hotel and Ballroom.

Previously, would-be dancers entered the ballroom by way of office. Patrons can now queue up the hotel. Now a new entrance has been provided and again multi-coloured stone work and wrought iron are prominent in the top.

balcony entrance and the ticket office. Patrons can now queue up beneath the shelter of a veranda which is dominated by two pillars of stone with lanterns fitted on the top.

Dancers entering the ballroom will have a clear view of the dance floor but will be prevented from making their way directly onto the floor by plush seating extending along the entrance way and a small wrought iron gate.

Along the carpeted walk, they will make their way to the ladies' and gents' cloakrooms and from there the ladies will make their way to the newly installed powder room. This will delight any girl and is both spacious and airy. Fitted with special 'dressing-table' make-up counters, the powder room will have two wall heaters for extra comfort and the spacious mirrors around the walls are being fitted with lighting. The blue and red and grey decorations are continued in the tiled floor which is in blue with red tiles scattered through the pattern.

important

"I think this room is just as important a feature as any other part of the ballroom," stated Mr. O'Donoghue as I admired the powder room.

And for that, being a woman with a 'thing' about powder rooms, I gave him full marks. All

(OVER TO OPPOSITE PAGE)

The Kerryman, 13 April 1963.

Tariff card, 1966.

GlenEagle Hotel, Killarney

TEL. 100

TARIFF 1966

HIGH SEASON: MAY 20—SEPT. 20

Bed and Breakfast	28/0
Bed and Breakfast (*with Bath*)	35/6

*

Daily	48/0
Daily (*with Bath*)	55/6

*

Weekly	294/0
Weekly (*with Bath*)	336/0

*

Luncheon	8/6
Dinner	15/6

*

LOW SEASON: SEPT. 20—MAY 20

Bed and Breakfast	25/0
Bed and Breakfast (*with Bath*)	33/6

*

Daily	42/0
Daily (*with Bath*)	49/6

*

Weekly	260/0
Weekly (*with Bath*)	275/0

*

Luncheon	8/6
Dinner	14/6

*

10% *Service Charge.*
25% *Reduction for Children under* 10 *years.*
Deposit for advance Booking £1 *per person.*

Sheila O'Donoghue, *proprietress.*

By January 1971 The Gleneagle Hotel consisted of a reception area, lounge, dining room, ballroom and thirty-six bedrooms.

The hotel's lobby in 1971.

Paddy and Sheila's daughter
Maura working at the hotel
reception in 1971.

The sun lounge, 1971.

The cocktail bar, a twin guestroom
and the Flesk Restaurant, 1971.

GLENEAGLE HOTEL KILLARNEY IRELAND

A Gleneagle Hotel dinner menu from 1969.

DINNER MENU

22nd April, 1969

Iced Melon Wedge
Fresh Grapefruit
Spaghetti Neapolitan

====

Consomme Brunoise
Cream of Celery

====

Grilled Dover Sole Maitre D'hotel
Fillets of Plaice a'la Orly
Roast Stuffed Turkey & Ham,
              Cranberry Sce.,
Minute Steak Garni
Grilled Pork Chop, Apple Sce.,
Lamb Cutlets Reforme

====

Creamed Cauliflower
Mashed & French Fried Potatoes

====

Fruit Trifle Chantilly
Coupe Mandarin

====

Coffee

Good Morning!

GlenEagle Hotel

Breakfast 8 — 10 a.m.

FRUIT JUICES
Chilled Tomato : Grapefruit : Orange

CEREALS
Porridge : Corn Flakes : Rice Crispies

EGGS
Boiled, Scrambled, Fried, Poached
or
GRILLS
Grilled Bacon, Egg, Sausage
Grilled Bacon, Egg, Tomato
Grilled Sausage, Tomato, Bacon
with
PRESERVES
Marmalade
with Tea or Coffee

A breakfast menu from the 1970s.

GlenEagle Hotel, Killarney

Full à la carte menu
from the 1970s.

a la carte

All orders take
approximately
20 minutes

hors d'oeuvres

Hors d'Oeuvres	5/6
Dublin Bay Prawn Cocktail	8/0
Smoked Salmon	9/6
Smoked Trout	7/0
Iced Melon Cup	3/6
Fresh Grapefruit	2/6
Assorted Fruit Juices	2/0

soups

Real Turtle Soup	5/0
Lobster Bisque	5/0
Soup of the Day	2/6
Cream of Asparagus	3/0
Consomme Marie-Celeste	3/0

Egg and Farinaceous Dishes

Omelettes:	Mushroom	5/0
	Savoury	5/0
	Plain	4/0
Spaghetti Napolitan		4/0
Macaroni au Gratin		4/0

fish

Whole Dover Sole (Grilled or Meuniere)	12/6
Fillets of Plaice a l'Anglaise	9/6
Medaillon of Turbot Dieppoise	10/6
Grilled Salmon Steak	14/6
Lobster Newburg (when available)	18/6
Cold Salmon Mayonnaise	12/6

entrees

Wiener Schnitzel	12/0
Escalope of Veal Holstein	13/6
Pork Chop Milanaise (2)	11/6
Chicken Maryland	14/0
Lamb Cutlets Princesse	10/6
Curried Chicken and Rice	12/6

beverages

Calypso Coffee	2/0
Pot of Coffee	2/0
Pot of Tea	2/6

grill

Choice Fillet Steak	(10-ozs.)	13/6
	(12-ozs.)	15/6
Sirloin Steak and Berbaise Sauce:	(10-ozs.)	12/0
	(12-ozs.)	14/0
Rump Steak	(10-ozs.)	11/0
	(12-ozs.)	13/0
Porterhouse Steak		14/0
Minute Steak		10/0
Chateau Briand (2 covers)		28/6
Lamb Cutlets (2)		10/6
Pork Chop (2)		11/6
Mixed Grill House Style		10/6
Lamb's Liver and Bacon		8/6

Joint from the Table d'Hotel Menu	12/0
Cold Chicken, Ham and Salad	13/0

vegetables

Potatoes Croquette	2/6
Potatoes Creamed or French Fried	2/0
Buttered Garden Peas	2/0
French Beans	2/6
Brussels Sprouts	2/6
Creamed Celery	2/6
Cauliflower or Spinach	3/0
Saute Onions	2/0
French Fried Onions	2/6
Saute Mushrooms	2/6

sweets

Crepes Suzette	10/6
Coupe Jacques	3/0
Peach Melba	3/6
Casata Milanaise	2/6
Dessert of the Day	2/6
Assorted Ices	2/0
Fresh Fruit Salad	5/6
Selection from Cheese Board	3/0
Tea, Bread and Butter, with any of the above items	2/6

10% Service Charge is added
to all accounts.

The famous Gleneagle Ballroom, first opened in 1959, was managed by Paddy's eldest son, Maurice. Throughout the 1960s The Gleneagle Hotel became synonymous with first-class dance bands, attracting punters from throughout Kerry and the adjoining counties. The ballroom and hotel were equipped with all the mod-cons of the time, including a new ventilation system that ensured the ballroom remained cool, and floodlighting equipment imported from Germany illuminated the car parks.

In the 1970s the ballroom featured a 50ft long mineral bar, offering ice-cream, teas, minerals and sandwiches.

The ballroom, with the stage visible in the foreground. To this day, the maple-sprung floor is considered one of the best dance floors in the country.

The ballroom set up with conference facilities in 1971.

The Gleneagle Hotel front
entrance, 1971.

Turning the sod on The Gleneagle Pitch and Putt
prior to its opening in April 1971 were Paddy Doyle
and Jimmy O'Meara. This marked a new chapter
in the hotel's expansion as Maurice O'Donoghue
began rapidly developing the hotel's leisure
facilities. The hotel would soon become renowned
for its recreational facilities. (© Kevin Coleman)

The Mill Road entrance
to the hotel, 1971.

The official opening of The Gleneagle Pitch and Putt Club, officiated by the Parliamentary Secretary to the Minister for Education, Mr Michael O'Kennedy, 25 April 1971. (© Kevin Coleman)

Paddy and his younger son Padraig O'Donoghue pictured at the official opening of the Pitch and Putt. (© Kevin Coleman)

Teeing-off at The Gleneagle Pitch and Putt in the 1970s.
(© Kevin Coleman)

In its heyday The Gleneagle Pitch and Putt Club featured two eighteen-hole courses. The grounds were originally owned by entomologist Edwin Bullock, renowned for his extensive insect collection.

(© Kevin Coleman)

The Kerryman,
24 April 1971.

Laying the foundations for the squash courts were
Dan Cooper, John Joe Harty, Paddy Doyle, Florence
O'Donoghue, Maurice O'Donoghue and Neilie
O'Sullivan. The squash courts at The Gleneagle, which
opened in 1972, were the first in Kerry and heralded the
beginning of the squash era in Killarney. Locals Denis
Geaney and Con Clifford played the very first game in
Kerry on The Gleneagle Courts in 1972. (© Kevin Coleman)

In 1975 two outdoor
tennis courts were added.
They were officially opened
in June of that year. (© Kevin
Coleman)

The first Gleneagle Squash
Committee pictured in
1978. (© Kevin Coleman)

Workmen putting the finishing touches to the two new tennis courts at the Gleneagle Pitch and Putt Club, Killarney.

CONTINUED EXPANSION AT GLENEAGLE

New tennis and billiards facilities add to present attractions

AND FROM this Saturday GlenEagle Hotel's Country Club comes into its own the official opening of two new tennis courts and laying on of a championship billiards table. As well as another championship is being installed in the body of the Hotel itself s the way.

th its latest additions, the Eagle is unequalled any-e in the county for the pro- of top-class indoor and or sporting facilities.

eady the GlenEagle has red a widespread reputa- for its 18 holes champion- Pitch and Putt course and fine squash courts— nly ones to be found any- e in Kerry.

w the management has up with further develop- which should attract still people to the firmly-esta- d Killarney centre.

e are providing another ty for Killarney," says J. oderick, recently-appointed tions Officer at the Glen-

"We feel that our two hardcourts and the two ionship tables for bil- and snooker should pro- ded amenities to the fac- already available here.

"The emphasis is on Club membership which provides excellent value. As well as single membership we also offer family and ladies' membership. Television coverage in recent times has definitely created a climate for this type of promotion. We feel that the tennis facilities are a rarity at the moment."

Intending members please note: you can have inclusive Single Membership for tennis, squash and Pitch and Putt for £15, or an individual fee of £3, £10 and £5 respectively; you can have inclusive Family Membership for tennis, squash and Pitch and Putt for £20, or an individual fee of £5, £15 and £7.50 respectively; you can have

inclusive Ladies' Membership for tennis, squash and Pitch and Putt for £12.50, or an individual fee of £3, £7.50 and £3.50 respectively.

Choice

The GlenEagle also offers you the choice of using their Par 3 18-hole golf course.

"Squash has been our big attraction," says J. J. Broderick, an Abbeyfeale man with wide experience of the showband and entertainment scene. "Club membership for this is very attractive and the same applies for our Pitch and Putt.

"Our new clubhouse or pavilion is ideally located beside the hotel. Patrons can have refreshments here and, of course, the Eagle's Nest Bar is just across the way. Another advantage is the fact that sports equipment and gear is available on a hire basis.

"Everybody is catered for— the professional and the beginner. There is no need for the beginner to lay out big money when he can have it here for a few pence.

"Non members are welcome but naturally members get prio-

rity. Our slogan is 'be a member.' The Gle the entertainment ce Kerry. There is no one p can offer so much. You many things contained one grounds—accomm food, drink and a f cabaret."

Cabaret

There is a club mem of 150 for Pitch and Putt 100 for squash.

There will be nightly and dancing in the G during July and Augus the old maestro Joe Los ing the summer season urday, July 5. Other 'big in the entertainment wo also being lined up at p

"The GlenEagle leads both as a hotel and as centre with every possibl ing facility," says Mr. O'Donoghue, proprieto Managing Director of th Eagle.

In the weeks and ahead many hundreds of uninitiated sporting folk able to see and enjoy the derful facilities at first h

GLENEAGLE

Hotel & Country Club

KILLARNEY

Par 3 Golf

8 hole, 1,400 yards
ar 3 Course.
xcellent Greens.

* Beautiful surroundings.
* A challenge to Golfers.
* Enjoyment for all

The GlenEagle Hotel, Killarney—a fine hotel with many attractions—not least of which is its beautiful setting.

The GlenEagle – a good hotel for many reasons

by Ian O'Leary

THE GlenEagle Hotel in Killarney is definitely the place to go to these days if you want a holiday full of " diversion " or even if one only wants to spend a few hours in pleasant company, relaxing or going through the rigours of one of the fastest games in the world.

For the GlenEagle has developed its own Country Club, and this provides luxurious comfort in the hotel for those who just wish to laze around, or for the more energetic there is squash and pitch and putt.

Eagle's Nest

And on this Friday for the " laze about fraternity," another facility is being added to the Country Club with the opening of the Eagle's Nest Bar. And of course it will prove extremely useful for those exhausted from their stint on the squash courts and wishing to replenish their fluid losses.

This new bar will be open of course to the general public and is situated right beside the squash courts and will in fact be the service area for these two championship standard courts. Such things as bookings, provision of racquets, etc., will be handled from the " Eagle's Nest."

Patio

Entry to the bar is from the large car park off the Mill Road. On parking your car you are immediately struck by the impressive Spanish Arch Patio incorporating the main entrance to the ballroom at one end, and the entrance to the squash courts and Eagle's Nest Bar at the other end.

Walking off the tiled patio you enter a large foyer with exit to the left to the main hotel building, to the right to the squash courts, showers and toilets, and straight ahead the entrance to the Eagle's Nest bar.

Entrance to the bar is through a beaten glass panelled door and I was immediately struck by the spaciousness of the room and the rich sumptuous look of the furnishings.

One of the aspects of the decor which intrigued me was the series of inverted conical shapes which formed the ceiling. These seven inverted cones form a pattern over the entire room with attractive lighting hanging from the centre of each cone. There is also an elaborate system of beams and pillars in Columbian pine contouring the inverted cones. This ceiling was designed by O'Flynn, Green and Buchan, architects.

Old prints

On the walls hang old prints of Killarney, all over 100 years old, and a series of prints of cock fighting. One wall of the room has been completely curtained to give a warm intimate atmosphere.

Carpeting throughout is in a rich floral design with a brown predominance to match the brown and cream upholstered furniture.

The bar is a split-level room, and on the lower level it is intended to have colour T.V. for patrons and customers. And on the occasions of parties or small weddings the carpet can be rolled up in this lower level area to provide a small dance floor.

You don't have to be a fitness addict or even a par three golfer to sample the cuisine of the Eagle's Nest Bar this winter, because it will be the main bar of the hotel, while the other bar in the actual hotel premises undergoes a face lift.

The GlenEagle is a privately owned family operated hotel, which, since the O'Donoghue family acquired it some 20 years ago, has developed into one of the foremost hotels in the area. For many years it has provided the main ballroom for the dancing scene in Kerry, and in later years has been developing its facilities for use, not only by hotel guests, but also by the people of Killarney. These facilities include pitch and putt, par three golf, and more recently two squash courts.

The O'Donoghue family are to be congratulated on the foresight with which they bring about the developments on their property. The Eagle's Nest Bar is the latest addition to the facilities and well worth a visit, or many visits.

The Gleneagle Hotel was a hive of
activity, so much so that *Gleneagle News*,
the hotel's very own newspaper,
was produced in the 1970s.

In account with . . .   Telephone No. 31870

The GlenEagle Hotel

LAKES OF KILLARNEY

ROOM NO. 42 ...... M. R. + Mrs. Demphy:

Month Sept. 17th – 24th 7 nights. (1972)
Brt. forward, £
Accom, per week 40 · 00
Morning Tea.
Bed/Breakfast
Luncheons
Dinners
High Teas
Tea, Coffee, Milk
Wines & Spirits
Teas
Tours
Sundries

Weekly Full Board £20 each.

Daily Total C/F £ 40 · 00 ·

10% Service Charge
Government Tax

GRAND TOTAL

Cr. Deposit Paid

NETT TOTAL

A bill for a seven-night stay with full board
in The Gleneagle Hotel in 1972.

GLENEAGLE

- DANCING • SOCIALS • HOTEL
- PITCH & PUTT • SQUASH

NEWS

gle's Nest for a Quiet Drink

ORMAL opening at the end of September of a new bar in the Glen Eagle was in
with the character of the Eagle's Nest — refined and elegant with the services
This latest addition to the Glen Eagle Country Club is quickly becoming a
night spot.

e have a private bar
ilable at any time for a
k. It is separate from
on area and is available
r the individual looking
k, for somebody on the
a dance or social, or
using the pitch and
se or the squash courts.
ature of the new bar is
cal shaped ceiling with
eriod style lighting. The
impression of spacious-
intimacy is interesting.
photographs show the
est has plenty of room.
out in such a way to
oups to sit around pri-
to widen into a larger

party or, if you want, to sit on
your own at the bar counter and
have a quiet drink or watch
colour television.

Around the walls there are
some fine old prints of Killarney
and on the floor there is soft,
deep carpet. The quiet subtlety
of the colour scheme achieves a
very soothing effect.

The ceiling was designed by
O'Flynn and Green architects
Cork. Credit for the magnificent
mahogany bar counter and back
panelling and for the very high
standard of workmanship in
building the Eagle's Nest must be
given to Nially O'Sullivan and
Florry O'Donoghue, two of the

The mahogany counter and back panelling, Irish tweed curtains
old prints in the Eagle's Nest bar.

Glen Eagle construction staff.
"Where did they get the space
from" is a general re-action from
those going into the new bar.
The Eagle's Nest is placed almost
in the centre of all of their enter-
prises at the Glen Eagle — just
off the car-park its the closest
point in the hotel to the pitch and
putt course, it's beside the
squash courts, the entrance to

the ballroom is just along
covered way and the hote
ception and dining room is
the corridor — the Eagle's
is the night place to go.

Since the other week a c
bar and snack service has s
in the Eagle's Nest. As a
pitch and putt and squash
patrons are increasingly usi
bar during the day.

ortable easy chairs, attractive setting . . . and colour television
at the Eagle's Nest bar.

ngo—Charge More?

Y DON'T YOU charge a £1
d increase your prizes" is
of the questions that has
put to us a number of times
tly about bingo at the Glen

have been running bingo

First bingo and then a dance. At
60p its good value.

We feel that many of our customers wouldn't like us to change
from this. However we are open
to suggestions — let us know
what you would like us to do.

GLEN EAGLE NEWS - NEW PA

THIS IS the first edition of the
Glen Eagle News. It is hoping to
give all the news about what is
happening at the Glen Eagle —
a calendar with the dances and
socials, news about pitch and
putt competitions, new developments (like the Eagle's Nest
bar), the latest situation in the
squash club, bingo results and
anything else that we think would
be of interest for our customers
and potential customers.

In this first edition we have
given you the news as we see it.
The Glen Eagle News will be published regularly and in future
editions we hope you will tell us
the kind of thing you would like

things that you think we
improve on.

Let us know about the
bands that you think we
be getting, about any
sporting facilities that yo
we should have. We w
space for your views in t
editions.

There's a lot going or
Glen Eagle at the mome
want to make sure that
of you as possible get t
about the action. We a
that it will encourage yo
more in contact with us.
running a business but
to try and make sure
many people as possible

Built in early 1974, The Eagle's Nest Bar became the social hub of the hotel. It was ideally situated at the centre of the hotel's leisure facilities and adjacent to the ballroom.

The Eagle's Nest had a number of interesting design aspects including conical-shaped ceilings designed by O'Flynn and Green Architects from Cork. The in-house carpentry team, Neilie O'Sullivan and Florence O'Donoghue, built the impressive mahogany bar counter.

Gleneagle Hotel Killarney

By the mid-1970s The Gleneagle Hotel had sixty-four bedrooms, all adjacent to the original building. The hotel's ever-increasing size required an innovative marketing campaign as illustrated in this brochure from the decade.

The Glen Eagle Hotel, Killarney.

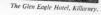

Spacious foyer looking out towards the Lower Lake and the Killarney mountains.

Gleneagle Hotel

There's an old Irish tradition called contentment. You get your first inkling of it the moment you enter the Glen Eagle Hotel. Bright smiles greet you. We are a family business. We care very much for our customers. Things function smoothly and with happy dignity. We offer you a hotel with 64 bedrooms. Elegantly furnished and with central heating. The Glen Eagle is spacious, comfortable, and with ample facilities—for families large or small ; young and not so young. The dining-room is opulent ; the food excellent, and the service is friendly. Efficient, too. At the Glen Eagle Hotel you are made welcome—not just as a tourist, but for yourself a person.

GLENEAGLE HOTEL

KILLARNEY, IRELAND
TEL. (064) 31870

This marketing campaign also included creating special package-holidays aimed at attracting visitors from Ireland and beyond.

INFORMATION SHEET

SPECIAL PACKAGE HOLIDAYS

More Information and Booking:

PACKAGE PROMOTIONS,
GLENEAGLE HOTEL,
KILLARNEY,
IRELAND.
Tel. (064) 31870

.....PITCH-AND-PUTT...........SQUASH...........

..........TENNIS.........DANCING.........FISHING

..TABLE TENNIS.....................CABARET......

............COLOUR T.V.............PAR 3 GOLF....

.....HOLIDAYS......HOLIDAYS.....HOLIDAYS...

KPW LTD.

...NTING CARS

...horse drawn car is one of the unique characteristics ...iated with Killarney. This kind of transport was used ...ally in Ireland up to twenty or thirty years ago. It has ...retained here to travel into some of the most scenic ...in the world (at a leisurely pace). ...: Two hours trip £2.80; (for four people) ...Half day trip £4.00; (for four people)

...TING

...ney is famous for its three lakes and these can best ...en from a boat. It is possible to arrange boating trips ...on to different islands or places of scenic interest. It is ...possible to arrange more extended excursions or to ...fishing trips.

...NTAIN CLIMBING & WALKING

...ng west from the GlenEagle one can see the ...licuddy Reeks (the highest mountain range in Ireland). ...leeks range (which includes Carrantuohill the 3,414 feet ...st mountain in Ireland), and many of the other peaks ...rovide pleasant hours of walking and climbing. Within ...g distance of the GlenEagle there are extensive areas ...odland, lakeside and forest, as well as the many nature ...in Killarney's National Park. This is an ideal location for ...dy who likes to spend time on foot. These are also ...ttractive areas for the photographer or the artist.

...NIS

...courts.

...RING

...f the truly memorable experiences of Killarney is the ...ip by Jaunting Car, pony and boat that travels by the ...hore, through the spectacular Gap of Dunloe rift valley ...rough Killarney's Three Lakes. ...ll as by jaunting car, pony and boat it is possible to see ...illarney Valley very effectively from a bicycle and these ...vailable for hire locally. ...are cars for hire, a local taxi service and the Killarney ...can be seen by Bus during the Summer months.

...NTS & ANIMALS

...Killarney area is famous for many things. The plant and ...l life of the area is particularly worth seeing. The ...colourful times of the year are the middle of May to the ...e of June, and from the end of September to the end ...tober, with the sharp freshness of Spring and the many ...s of brown in Autumn. Here are the only herd of Irish ...Deer that still remain—there are 200 red deer and ...sika, or Jap deer, in the Killarney area. Over eighty ...s of birds were listed around Killarney in a recent ...twelve month period.

SPECIAL HOLIDAY OFFERS FROM THE GLENEAGLE

The following is a series of extra attractive holiday offers from the GlenEagle which will enable you to enjoy all of the facilities we have described at very competitive prices.
Note: (the following apply to all of the holidays in this section).

1. **FAMILY OFFERS:**
   (a) Children accompanying parents.
   — Under 4 years (staying in parents bedroom) free.
   — Under 10 years reduction of 50%.
   — Under 15 years reduction of 25%.
   (b) Babysitting facilities available.
2. The prices quoted below are net and include service charge and all Government taxes.

3. **SUPPLEMENTS:**
   (a) Private bath per person—50p week-end; £2.00 per week.
   (b) Single Room—per week £4.00 (low season); £6.00 (high season).
   Single room—per week-end £1.00 (low season); £1.50 (high season).

4. The season at the GlenEagle is divided into two: July and August is the high season and the rest of the year is low season.

5. Special prices for periods not included below are also available.

GAME BALL HOLIDAY

The hotel sporting and entertainment facilities are included in the package price—squash, par 3 golf, pitch-and-pu[tt], dancing, fishing, children's playground etc.
PRICE: High Season—July and August.
   Week-end £8.00 (Friday Dinner to Sunday Lunch).
   Week £26.00 (All meals and accommodation for sev[en] days).
PRICE: Low Season—Rest of Year.
   Week-end £7.50 (Friday Dinner to Sunday Lunch).
   Week £23.00 (All meals and accommodation for sev[en] days).

GOLFING HOLIDAY

This includes green fees at Killarney's two 18-hole la[ke] side championship courses. Free golfing on the GlenEagle P[ar] 3 Pitch-and-Putt courses. All of the facilities (detailed und[er] Game Ball Holiday) are included in the package price.
PRICE: High Season—July and August.
   Week-end £10.20 (Friday Dinner to Sunday Lunch pl[us] two days green fees).
   Week £32.00 (Green fees plus all meals and acco[m]modation for seven days).
PRICE: Low Season—Rest of Year.
   Week-end £9.70 (Friday Dinner to Sunday Lunch pl[us] two days green fees).
   Week £29.00 (Green fees plus all meals and acco[m]modation for seven days).

SQUASH HOLIDAY

Two courts in the hotel are available for guests (there is [a] small lighting charge as is usual for this game). Equipme[nt] available for hire. (Par 3 Golf, Pitch-and-Putt, Dancin[g] Children's playing ground and other hotel facilities are inclu[d]ed in package price).
PRICE: High Season—July and August.
   Week-end £8.00 (Friday Dinner to Sunday Lunc[h]).
   Week £26.00 (All meals and accommodation for 7 day[s]).
PRICE: Low Season—Rest of Year.
   Week-end £7.50 (Friday Dinner to Sunday Lunc[h]).
   Week £23.00 (All meals and accommodation for 7 day[s]).

PITCH-AND-PUTT & PAR 3 GOLF PACKAGE

One 18-hole championship Pitch-and-Putt and 18-hole Par [3] courses. Two quite distinct courses are laid out on twe[nty] two acres of gently rolling, wooded parkland. Other ho[tel] facilities—squash, table tennis, dancing, tennis and so on [—] are also available to guests availing of this holiday.
PRICE: High Season—July and August.
   Week-end £8.00 (Friday Dinner to Sunday Lunch).
   Week £25.00 (All meals and accommodation for sev[en] days).
PRICE: Low Season—Rest of Year.
   Week-end £7.50 (Friday Dinner to Sunday Lunc[h]).
   Week £23.00 (All meals and accommodation for sev[en] days).

LEARN HOW TO FISH HOLIDAY

Many would-be anglers never get to handle a rod because they don't know where to begin. As well many anglers never get as much enjoyment out of fishing as they might because they don't know how to prepare their equipment properly, or don't know how to go about the business of fishing in the way it should be done. This is why we have decided to run this "Learn How to Fish Holiday". Our instructor will give instructions on fly tying, bait preparation, in preparing casts and rods and in storing equipment. He will also spend periods on the bank of the river giving lessons in casting, using a net and so on. The other hotel facilities are included in the price of this package.
PRICE: High Season—July and August.
   Week-end £10.00 (Friday Dinner to Sunday Lunch).
PRICE: Low Season—Rest of Year.
   Week-end £9.50 (Friday Dinner to Sunday Lunch).

DANCING

This is a holiday for anybody who is keen to take the floor but is particularly suited to either week or week-end in the summer time or week-ends in the winter. This is mentioned because during the winter period dancing only takes place on Friday and Sunday nights. The biggest dancing attractions in Ireland play to the GlenEagle patrons. This is one of the most sophisticated ballrooms in the country and has for over thirteen years been the most popular venue in this part of the country. The other hotel facilities—squash, Par 3 golf, pitch-and-putt, croquet, table tennis and so on—are included in this package price.
PRICE: High Season—July and August.
   Week-end £8.00 (Friday Dinner to Sunday Lunch).
   Week £26.00 (All meals and accommodation for seven days).
PRICE: Low Season—Rest of Year.
   Week-end £7.50 (Friday Dinner to Sunday Lunch).
   Week £23.00 (All meals and accommodation for seven days).

TARIFF 1973

	HIGH SEASON (JUNE, JULY and AUGUST)	LOW SEASON (Rest of Year)
Bed and Breakfast	£2.00	£1.80
Bed and Breakfast with Bath	£2.30	£2.10
Daily (Full Board)	£3.80	£3.50
Daily (Full Board) with Bathroom	£4.10	£3.80
Dinner, Bed and Breakfast	£3.10	£3.10
Dinner, Bed and Breakfast with Bath	£3.40	£3.30
Weekly (Full Board)	£23.00	£21.00
Weekly (Full Board) with Bath	£25.00	£23.00
Weekly, Dinner, Bed and Breakfast	£22.00	£19.00
Weekly, Dinner, Bed and Breakfast with Bath	£23.00	£21.00
Luncheon		80p
Dinner		£1.30

Not less than three days — applies to Daily (Full Board), Daily (Full Board) with Bathroom, Dinner, Bed and Breakfast, Dinner, Bed and Breakfast with Bath

10% Service Charge.
Deposit of £1.00 per person for advance booking.
Reduction for Children on application.

Enquiries and bookings:
PACKAGE PROGRAMMES, GLENEAGLE HOTEL, KILLARNEY, IRELAND.   TEL. (064) 31870.

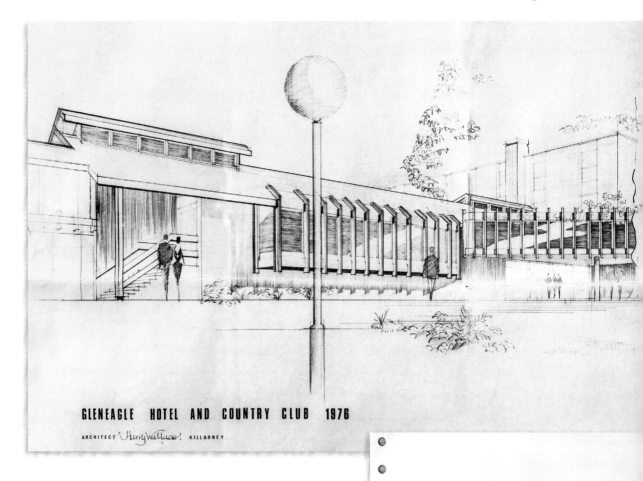

GLENEAGLE HOTEL AND COUNTRY CLUB 1976

ARCHITECT *Harry Wallace* KILLARNEY.

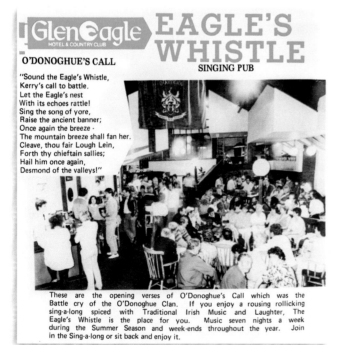

EAGLE'S WHISTLE
SINGING PUB

GlenEagle HOTEL & COUNTRY CLUB

O'DONOGHUE'S CALL

"Sound the Eagle's Whistle,
Kerry's call to battle.
Let the Eagle's nest
With its echoes rattle!
Sing the song of yore,
Raise the ancient banner;
Once again the breeze ·
The mountain breeze shall fan her.
Cleave, thou fair Lough Lein,
Forth thy chieftain sallies;
Hail him once again,
Desmond of the valleys!"

These are the opening verses of O'Donoghue's Call which was the Battle cry of the O'Donoghue Clan. If you enjoy a rousing rollicking sing-a-long spiced with Traditional Irish Music and Laughter, The Eagle's Whistle is the place for you. Music seven nights a week during the Summer Season and week-ends throughout the year. Join in the Sing-a-long or sit back and enjoy it.

The bar was called after the traditional marching tune of the O'Donoghue Clan.

Name of Premises: GLENEAGLE HOTEL   Addre

	OVERNIG ROOM ONLY	
	Single £	Doub £
1 Jun–31 Dec Bank Holiday Wkends	~~~~	~~~~
1 Apr–31 May	~~~~	~~~~
1 Jan–31 Mar		

A full Irish breakfast is included in the

In 1976, due to the ever-increasing size and popularity of the hotel, a new bar was built to cater for locals and visitors alike. The Eagle's Whistle was designed by Architect Harry Wallace and featured a billiards room with five championship-sized snooker tables. (© Harry Wallace)

The Kerryman,
2 July 1976.

Bord Fáilte tariff card from 1978.

RD FAILTE EIREANN

Maximum Charges
(Inclusive of Value Added Tax)

S ROAD KILLARNEY CO KERRY

Year for which charges apply **1978**

	PRIVATE BATH		DAILY INCLUSIVE (3 or more days)		WEEKLY INCLUSIVE		Breakfast P=Plain F=Full	TABLE D'HOTE			Reduction for Children	Service Charge
					Full Board	Part Board						
T	Single £	Double £	Single £	Double £	Single £	Single £	£	Lunch £	High Tea £	Dinner £	%	%
.00	1.50					70.80		2.80		4.80		10.0
.40	1.50					61.20		2.40		4.20		10.0
.40	1.50					57.00		2.20		4.00		10.0

IT IS HEREBY CERTIFIED that the charges as set out above are Maximum Charges for the period stated and are in accordance with the Requirements of the Tourist Traffic Acts 1939-1972 and the Prices Control Acts 1958-1972.

e prices above.

J. A. FLANNERY, Bord Failte Eireann

Advertisement
in *The Kerryman*,
15 October 1976.

In the winter of 1977 work commenced on a brand-new wing of forty-eight bedrooms. Three floors opened in May 1978 and the fourth floor opened the following year. (© Don MacMonagle, macmonagle.com)

In 1979 a new dome-shaped function room was built. Originally called The Celebrity Club, this room would cater for weddings, socials and conferences as well as being a late-night entertainment venue. The GAA Annual Congress took place here in 1981. (© Don MacMonagle, macmonagle.com)

In account with . . .

The GlenEagle Hotel AND COUNTRY CLUB
LAKES OF KILLARNEY

Telephone (064)31870

ROOM NO.......... M..........	O'DONOGHUE & O'KEEFE WEDDING RECEPTION				
Month 7/09/1982					
Brt. forward, £					
Accom. per week					
Morning Tea	169 @ £10.00		£1,690.00		
Bed/Breakfast					
Luncheons	SHERRY RECEPTION:				
Dinners	10 Sherry		£80.00		
High Teas	84 Orange		£33.60		
Tea, Coffee, Milk					
Wine & Spirits	TABLE DRINKS:				
Teas	24 White Wine		£120.00		
Tours	18 Red Wine		£117.00		
Sundries	16 V. de Vernay		£128.00		
	12 Orange		£ 18.00		
	1 V. de Clinquet		£ 15.00		
		£1,690.00 £511.60		£2,201.60	
	10% Service Charge			£ 220.16	
	FULL TOTAL:			£2,421.76	
Daily Total C/F					
10% Service Charge					
GRAND TOTAL					
DEPOSIT PAID					
NET TOTAL	£2,421.76				

A bill to wine and dine 169 wedding guests in The Celebrity Club at The Gleneagle Hotel in 1982.

In 1988 a floating bar was installed in The Celebrity Club. As well as being a popular wedding venue the room doubled as Wings Niteclub.
(© Don MacMonagle, macmonagle.com)

GLENEAGLE HOTEL *has 100 bedrooms, all with private Bath/Shower in Suite, Direct Dial Phone and most with Colour Television.*

A brochure for
The Gleneagle Hotel in 1986.

The Mill Road entrance
of The Gleneagle Hotel
in 1986. (© Don MacMonagle,
macmonagle.com)

Checking in at the hotel's
reception in the 1990s.

By the early 1990s Maurice was ready to commence work on his next big project. He had planned on adding a swimming pool to the hotel's facilities since the late 1960s and finally in 1991 his vision was realised. (© Don MacMonagle, macmonagle.com)

The Gleneagle Hotel in 1990. In this year a further forty-eight bedrooms were opened. These new rooms, along with the existing balcony rooms, were serviced by the hotel's first lift which was installed in 1988.

Maurice O'Donoghue and builder Pat O'Connor oversee the digging of the foundations of The Aquila Club in 1990. (© Don MacMonagle, macmonagle.com)

Maurice O'Donoghue pictured in front of the foundations for the Aquila Club. While the concrete frame of the swimming pool was settling, construction began on a further thirty-three bedrooms.

(© Don MacMonagle, macmonagle.com)

Taoiseach Charles Haughey officially opens the Aquila Club, 8 November 1991. The leisure centre's name derives from the Latin word for eagle. (© Michelle Cooper-Galvin)

Taoiseach Charles Haughey cutting the ribbon at the opening of the Aquila Club, 8 November 1991.

(© Michelle Cooper-Galvin)

In 1993 the hotel's lobby and main entrance were extended and a new reception desk was built.

In the same year,
the Aquila Club was
also extended to include
a new billiards room,
crèche, beauty salon,
hairdressers and gym.

What had previously been the billiards room became a brand-new à la carte restaurant.
Artist's impression for O'D's Restaurant, 1996.

In 1996 a further twenty-three bedrooms and the hotel's vast laundry were built.

In May 1999 construction began on Maurice's most ambitious project yet. Ireland's National Events Centre, or the INEC as it is now known, cost in the region of £5 million to construct and, with no grant aid, was entirely funded by the family-run business. It was the biggest venue of its kind outside of Dublin and it was envisioned that its flexible design would attract conferences, conventions and concerts that were previously confined to the capital. Pictured at the turning of the sod were Maurice O'Donoghue, TD John O'Donoghue, Senator Paul Coughlan and TD Jackie Healy-Rae.
(© Don MacMonagle, macmonagle.com)

The INEC was officially opened by An Taoiseach Bertie Ahern in June 2000. In his speech the Taoiseach said the project was a credit to the O'Donoghues who had invested time and money to transform The Gleneagle over the past forty years. Mr Ahern said the family could proudly claim to have more amenities than any other hotel in the country. (© *The Kerryman*, 9 June 2006. Photo © Don MacMonagle, macmonagle.com)

The state-of-the-art INEC has seating for over 2,000 people and can accommodate 3,500 for standing concerts. The seating, which cost over half a million pounds, was imported from America and its innovative design means it can be fully retracted. The venue is renowned in both conferencing and event circles for its flexibility, while its elaborate flying and trussing equipment is instrumental in staging large-scale theatre and concert productions.

Gleneagle continues €2.2m revamp

A €2.2 million refurbishment pro-gramme at the Gleneagle Hotel in Killarney is being continued into the New Year with extra work being carried out on the bedroom stock.

BY BREDA JOY

Patrick O'Donoghue

Between 2010 and 2012 over €2.2 million is being invested in refurbishing and improving facilities at the family-owned hotel. The cost of carpeting the public areas alone was over € 250,000.

"It is a sizeable investment but the money is being put to good use," Gleneagle MD Patrick O'Donoghue said.

"We get to improve our facilities while also pumping money into the local economy via contractors and suppliers."

By February 2012, 96 guestrooms will have been completely refurbished. The initial phase of refurbishment, consisting of 48 guestrooms, was completed in 2010.

The second phase of 24 balcony guestrooms was completed last December with an additional 24 balcony rooms due for completion by this February. A third phase, including 44 rooms, will be refurbished in 2013.

The hotel lobby, Green Room Lounge and Back Stage Bar have also been kitted out with new carpet, artworks, draperies, decoration and upgraded furniture.

Not all improvements are visible. Full Wi-Fi coverage is now in all conference areas and guestrooms.

This network can be enhanced for specialist conferences where a high density of delegates require simultaneous Wi-Fi access.

Kerry's Eye,
12 January 2012.

In 2014 The Gleneagle Hotel invested €300,000 in upgrading its Wi-Fi network. 'A reliable and robust Wi-Fi network is mandatory and this investment future-proofs our ability to host world-class national and international conferences and events,' said Patrick O'Donoghue. Patrick is pictured with Shane Hartigan, CEO of Integrated Media Solutions.

(© Valerie O'Sullivan)

True to the ethos of the late Paddy O'Donoghue who said, 'You have to keep on modernising your hotel. There is no point being timid,' the O'Donoghues continue to update and improve the hotel's facilities. The reception at The Gleneagle Hotel and the library which overlooks reception, 2015.

(© Andrew Bradley)

The layout and shape of the lounge remains unchanged since
the days of the original Flesk House. (© Andrew Bradley)

The Flesk Restaurant, 2015. (© Andrew Bradley)

The famous Green Room Bar. (© Andrew Bradley)

Room with a view. A balcony room at The Gleneagle Hotel. (© Andrew Bradley)

From humble beginnings as an eight-bedroom house, The Gleneagle Hotel has grown into one of Ireland's leading entertainment and leisure destinations. Since the new millennium, the complex expanded to include self-catering apartments and The Gleneagle's sister hotel, The Brehon. (© Valerie O'Sullivan)

CHAPTER TWO

Family and Staff

The Gleneagle Hotel is a true family affair. Generations of families holiday here, generations of families work here and three generations of one family have run the hotel since it first opened its doors.

In 1957 Paddy and Sheila O'Donoghue, along with their seven children, moved from their family home above Paddy's chemist in Main Street, Killarney to Flesk House on Muckross Road. Within months the young family set about welcoming paying guests and expanding and improving their fledgling business.

The O'Donoghues' entrepreneurial spirit came to the fore again in 1959, when they built a dance hall adjacent to the hotel. Their eldest son Maurice, who was studying pharmacy in Dublin at the time, drove home three to four nights a week to run dances. Maurice would never practice as a pharmacist; instead he embarked on a lifelong career in hospitality and entertainment. The courage and business acumen imbued in him by his parents, combined with his flair for recognising and harnessing new trends made him a leader in his field. Together with his wife Margaret, Maurice set about developing The Gleneagle into an all-inclusive holiday destination. For over forty years, they devised and designed new ways to attract visitors to Killarney.

The Gleneagle Hotel is now under the guardianship of the third generation of O'Donoghues; Maurice and Margaret's son Patrick and his wife Eileen. Sixty years and three generations on, the O'Donoghues continue to improve, expand and develop their family business.

Paddy O'Donoghue in the front room of the hotel shortly after its purchase in 1957. With no huge inheritance, Paddy attributed his great success in business to hard work, often working fifteen-hour days. 'I am and always have been a working man,' he said, 'Neither myself nor any member of my family have ever been afraid of hard work.'
(*The Kerryman*, 1 July 1961).

Paddy O'Donoghue the chemist at The Medical Hall, Killarney. Paddy attended The Presentation Monastery School in Killarney before going on to the St Brendan's College. He served as an apprentice chemist to Mr Hartnett in Henn Street (now Plunkett Street) before going on to UCD for his MPSI course.

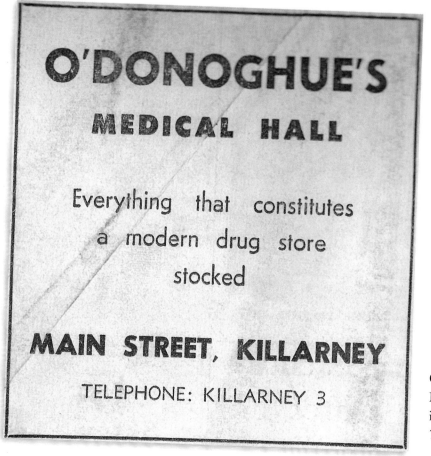

The Medical Hall, Main Street, Killarney. After he qualified, Paddy returned to Killarney to P.D. Foley's chemist shop, which he bought in 1926. In 1954, he extended the premises into O'Leary's Bar next door.

O'Donoghue's Medical Hall advertisement in the *Irish Independent*, 7 July 1969.

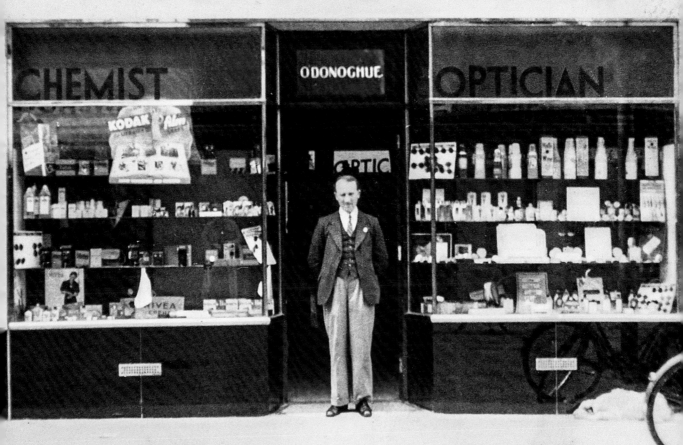

Paddy O'Donoghue outside Killaha Castle in his native Glenflesk. In naming their hotel, The Gleneagle, Paddy drew inspiration from his townland and from Killarney's long association with Ireland's native eagles.

The marriage of Paddy O'Donoghue and Sheila Foley in 1936. Sheila Foley was the daughter of Charles and Ellen Foley of Foley's Bar, New Street Killarney. Sheila's bridesmaid was Eileen Hardy who travelled especially from England for the occasion. Best man was Jim Flaherty, brother of Monsignor Hugh O'Flaherty.

Sheila O'Donoghue busy entertaining her seven children in 1950. Sheila lived her entire life in Killarney, moving from New Street to Main Street after she married in 1936 and then to Muckross Road following the purchase of Flesk House in 1957. From left, Bríd, Maurice, Aideen, Padraig, Sheila, Anne Marie, Eileen and Maura.

Paddy and Sheila O'Donoghue with comedians Tom and Paschal at the opening night of The Gleneagle Cabaret in June 1969. (© Don MacMonagle, macmonagle.com)

Telegram from the staff of The Gleneagle Hotel to
Maurice and Margaret O'Donoghue on the occasion
of their marriage in April 1964.

Dinner for Paddy's nephew, Father Noel Dermot O'Donoghue, with family and friends, at The Gleneagle Hotel.

Maurice and Margaret's daughters, Shella and Aine O'Donoghue, playing outside The Gleneagle Hotel in 1973. Upon having their own family, the young couple identified a gap in the market for family holidays. In the decades that followed, they developed The Gleneagle into one of Ireland's leading family-friendly hotels.
(© Donal MacMonagle, macmonagle.com)

Paddy O'Connor, Con O'Keeffe and the Gleneagle buses at the ready, July 1961. Con O'Keeffe joined The Gleneagle team in 1959, at the start of the entertainment era, while also holding down a full-time job in the shoe factory in Killarney. Con was a well-known face at The Gleneagle for over fifty-five years. He was Head Doorman for thirty years and later drove the hotel's wedding car and VIP guests.
(© Harry MacMonagle, macmonagle.com)

Old friends and work colleagues, Tom O'Sullivan, Con O'Keeffe, and Maurice O'Donoghue. Both Tom and Con joined Maurice and The Gleneagle team in 1959 and continued to work at the hotel until recent years.

In June 1980, Gay Byrne brought his concert tour to The Gleneagle Hotel: the show's featured artists included Sandi Jones, Tom and Paschal and Larry Cunningham.

Johnny Logan, fresh after his win for Ireland at the Eurovision Song Contest 1980, is pictured with Maurice O'Donoghue at The Gleneagle Hotel. (© Don MacMonagle, macmonagle.com)

Maurice and Margaret O'Donoghue with Gleneagle-favourite Joe Cuddy and Eurovision winner Johnny Logan. (©Don MacMonagle, macmonagle.com)

Maurice O'Donoghue and his son Patrick with comedian Brendan O'Carroll and Gleneagle Marketing Manager Marie Quinlivan at The Gleneagle Hotel in 1995. (© Don MacMonagle, macmonagle.com)

The Gleneagle team outside the hotel in 1997. (© Valerie O'Sullivan)

The Gleneagle staff from down through the years, pictured at an event to celebrate the 40th anniversary of the hotel.

World-famous Irish actress Maureen O'Hara attends The Brendan Grace Show while holidaying in Killarney. She is pictured here with Sheila O'Donoghue, Brendan Grace and his daughter Melanie.

(© Eamonn Keogh, macmonagle.com)

Late night at The Gleneagle Hotel. Nanci Griffith pictured with Eileen and Patrick
O'Donoghue after her performance at the INEC. (© Don MacMonagle, macmonagle.com)

Patrick, Peter, Margaret and Eileen O'Donoghue at the official opening of the INEC in
June 2000. (© Michelle Cooper Galvin)

Maurice O'Donoghue listens to
country singer Charlie Pride at
the first ever concert in the INEC.

(© Don MacMonagle, macmonagle.com)

Tony Fenton and the 2FM Roadshow visiting The Gleneagle Hotel to celebrate forty
years in business. (© Valerie O'Sullivan)

Kris Kristofferson chats with Patrick and Aine O'Donoghue before performing to a packed audience at the INEC in June 2005. (© Valerie O'Sullivan)

American singer-songwriter Kenny Rogers with Patrick O'Donoghue before his performance at the INEC in July 2013. (© Valerie O'Sullivan)

Minister John O'Donoghue officially opens The Brehon, November 2004. The Minister is pictured here with members of The O'Donoghue family, from right: Eamon, Aoife, Aine, Margaret, Patrick, Sheila, John, Shella, Eileen and Maurice. (© Valerie O'Sullivan)

Fourth generation. Sheila O'Donoghue pictured with her great-grandchild Niamh O'Donoghue at the opening of The Brehon. (© Don MacMonagle, macmonagle.com)

Michael Flatley pictured with brothers Patrick and John O'Donoghue in February 2007.
(© Valerie O'Sullivan)

Sheila O'Donoghue and her grandson Patrick greeting the President of Ireland, Mary McAleese and her husband Dr Martin McAleese at The Gleneagle Hotel in August 2007. (© Valerie O'Sullivan)

Sheila O'Donoghue, holding her portrait that was commissioned by the Irish Hotels Federation in recognition of her lifelong contribution to the hospitality industry in Ireland. (© Eamonn Keogh, macmonagle.com)

More than fifty years after the O'Donoghues opened The Gleneagle Hotel, Sheila continued to play an active role in the business. She passed away in August 2011, aged 100 years.
(© Valerie O'Sullivan)

In 2004 over twenty-five different nationalities worked at The Gleneagle Hotel. Pictured, from left to right, are: Paul Ator (Canada), Aris Fadicah (Malaysia), Gosia Kowalska (Poland), Miriam Zahradnikova (Czech Republic), Marie Sinon (France), Matthew Linton-Ford (England), Cecilia Barkman (Sweden), Abdul Latifkhan (Bangladesh), Rob Wang Xjung (China), Tristan Pashaj (Albania). Second row: Aung Aung OO (Burma), Gurdip Singh (India), Klarika Roosipuu (Estonia), Sophia Stepbakova (Ukraine), Eilish Walsh (Ireland), Enkhee Dashmaa (Mongolia), Myrna Fllagia (Philippines), Mercedes Palenque (Spain), Alda Liverte (Latvia), Lynda Brinkmann (Australia), John Abbing (Netherlands), Edvardas Puotkalis (Lituania), Beatrix Badners (Germany), Jouni Siiriainen (Finland), Robert 'Pogo' Paterson (Scotland). (© Valerie O'Sullivan)

In 2012 The Gleneagle was awarded the Fáilte Ireland Optimus Mark of Best Practice in special recognition of their ongoing commitment to continuous improvement and a first-class customer experience.

(© Valerie O'Sullivan)

The Gleneagle truly is a family-run business with generations of Killarney families working day-to-day in the hotel. Pictured here, in August 2014, are five of these families. Sitting from left, Mrs Margaret O'Donoghue with her grandchildren, Peter and Eve O'Donoghue, Mrs Una O'Callaghan with her granddaughter Michelle O'Callaghan, Michael Carey and his granddaughter Karen Harrington. Back row: Tomás and Jamie O'Sullivan, grandsons of Tom O'Sullivan (missing from photo) and Con O'Keeffe with his granddaughter Danielle Weber. (© Valerie O'Sullivan)

Eileen, Eamon, Sinead, Margaret and Patrick O'Donoghue, at the Kerry branch of the Irish Hotels Federation Annual Ball in the Dromhall Hotel in December 2014. The O'Donoghues were presented with a special award marking over fifty years in the hospitality business.

(© Don MacMonagle, macmonagle.com)

Patrick and Eileen O'Donoghue outside The Gleneagle Hotel in April 2015. The couple are the third generation of O'Donoghues to run the family business. (© Don MacMonagle, macmonagle.com)

Staff of The Gleneagle Hotel in April 2015. (© Don MacMonagle, macmonagle.com)

Staff of The Gleneagle pictured
outside the hotel in April 2015.

(© Don MacMonagle, macmonagle.com)

CHAPTER THREE

Community and Tourism

The Gleneagle has always been much more than a hotel – it is a hub of creativity and new ideas. Festivals, visitor attractions, conferences and community initiatives are devised, developed and rolled out annually. The goal of the hotel has always been to provide its guests with more than just a room with a bed and so today it plays host to numerous festivals, concerts and events as well as offering its guests plenty to do come rain or shine. The hotel is also very much a part of the local community and has been involved in all sorts of sponsorships down through the years from The Gleneagle Concert Band to Killarney Summerfest.

Maurice and Tourism

Page 4 "The Kingdom" July 26 1988

Maurice O'Donoghue at 50:

A Man On The Move

FRANK LEWIS REPORTS

MAURICE O'DONOGHUE IN HAPPY MOOD.........

Maurice O'Donoghue gets nervous if he is in the one position for too long. He likes to be on the move. To come up with new ideas. Experiment with new things.

This Wednesday (July 27) Maurice O'Donoghue will be 50 - and his son Padraig, who works in the business with him will be 21.

Over the past thirty years O'Donoghue has radically changed the face of Killarney tourism and if it were not for his work the industry in Killarney would be very much poorer today.

In the mid fifties Killarney was perceived in Ireland as being a place where English - or increasingly at that time Americans - went on holiday. The Maurice O'Donoghue's concept of developing the GlenEagle as a major entertainment centre was revolutionary.

Gradually more and more Irish were attracted to Killarney and are now a most important part of the tourist mix coming to the resort.

Maurice's next move was to provide a whole range of sporting facilities on a twenty acre stretch of parkland at the GlenEagle - pitch and putt, par 3 golf, tennis and indoors squash and snooker.

"It was clear that the visitors weren't satisfied with four walls, a nice bed and good food...they wanted things to do during the day and at night - in wet or dry weather", O'Donoghue has the knack of looking through the eyes of the average tourist.

In '69 Maurice O'Donoghue was elected Chairman of the Killarney Urban District Council - he has been a member of the Council since 1967. He was chairman of the Council for the fourth time in 1987/88 and is current chairman of Killarney Tourism.

Through the years he has been involved in a series of imaginative sponsorships. Closest to his heart is the realisation of his dream to provide a brass and reed band for Killarney.

Other sponsorships have included making GlenEagle Basketball one of the country's super teams in this country, building the Rally of the Lakes to the most important event of its kind in the country - now poised to get world series status. The GlenEagle Cycling Club is another of his current sponsorships.

The purchase of Scotts Hotel, the development of the highly innovative all weather Scotts Beer Garden, the opening of the Irish Transport Museum, the provision of the Killarney Waterbus and the planning of Wings Nite Club at the GlenEagle.

"It has been clear to me over the past couple of years that our greatest need - and the greatest need of the entire tourist industry not only in Killarney but in the rest of Kerry as well - was the development of a professional packaging, marketing and handling agency". Out of this concern O'Donoghue developed Destination Killarney.

Destination Killarney's current campaign is daily getting 3/400 callers to their office at Scotts Gardens, 60/70 telephone calls and 40/50 written enquiries. In spite of the very noticable decrease in American visitors tourism in Killarney in 1988 is being significantly helped by Destination Killarney.

"We have among the finest tourist products in the world but the return we are getting from it, compared to what we could get is tiny. If we package what we have to offer attractively, market it effectively, and service it professionally tourism here in the 1990's will be unrecognisable", O'Donoghue says with absolute conviction.

The Kingdom, 26 July 1988.

At the age of forty-one Killarney born and based Maurice O'Donoghue has the distinction of being the only local business man involved in local politics. He is an active member of Killarney Urban District Council. But local politics is not the only string to O'Donoghue's bow — he is proprietor and Managing Director of Gleneagle Hotel and Country Club, Director of Killarney Race Company and since last year owner of Scotts Hotel in Killarney.

A tall, slim rangy man, with blonde/red hair, a crumpled smile and a lived-in face, his movements appear jointless as he hunches his shoulders forwards towards the future. To watch him stride his hotel complex, or listen to his half-bantering, wholly serious policy-making telephone conversations, the isolated loneliness of command sits heavy; but within the framework of his family, wife Margaret and five children, he is relaxed to the point of somnabulism.

His current penchants and enthusiasms are divided between his promotion of Killarney and South Kerry, which he says: "could be the greatest tourist resort in Western Europe" and further development of the Gleneagle, which under his auspices in little over 20 years has grown from a private Georgian House with eight bedrooms to a 90 bedroomed hotel, all with private baths and the development of a Country Club — "now the largest entertainment complex in Ireland which is regarded as the most prestigious venue in the country by leading Irish and international artistes."

Delving into the pros of Killarney and South Kerry's tourist attraction O'Donoghue states, "It has all the natural attractions, like mountains, lakes, woods and gardens. There are wonderful walks and everyone should hire a bicycle and ride around the lakes. The youth is becoming constantly more aware of the great beauty of Killarney". He explains that some twenty years ago, Killarney was a Mecca for British coaches and the starting age was 50 upwards! But on the positive marketing side he feels the continent must be courted; that big names like the late President de Gaulle and Princess Beatrix can only provide the right image; and that leisure activities like horse racing, golf and car racing should be promoted to the maximum.

Looking back with nostalgia to the '30s and '40s when developments like the 11,000 acre National Park,

Talking to
MAURICE O'DONOGHUE
THE MAN BEHIND GLENEAGLE HOTEL & COUNTRY CLUB

Country Club and Hotel run concurrently. In 1957 O'Donoghue's father, a veteran of the War of Independence bought the Gleneagle Hotel, on three acres of land; 1959 was the year when 12 bedrooms were added and when the function room for 200 cum dance hall (400) was built; and when Maurice O'Donoghue's entrepreneurial flair began gestation, triggered by the popularity of the Ag. dances and the advent of the showbands. He was studying to be a chemist at that time, but worked in the Gleneagle during the holidays. Throughout the early '60s, lounges, kitchens and thirty-eight new bedrooms were added and at the Country Club the ballroom was extended and refurbished, while entertainment developed from running dances only to Irish cabaret orientated towards tourists.

During the late '60s and early '70 British business collapsed as a result of the Northern Ireland troubles and rather than accept a depressed market

the building of the Fitzgerald Stadium G.A.A. Pitch, the Race Course and Killarney Golf Course were the result of united community endeavour, he feels private enterprise is no substitute. But projecting forward he enthuses about the formation of a tourist police force, whose main job would be the control of tourism answering queries, liaising between complaints and the law, which could equally come

from both sides. O'Donoghue saw a similar pilot scheme work successfully in Greece and he would envisage trained students, with languages, working on a part-time basis.

He returns to speak about the Gleneagle, perhaps with some reluctance, as he would appear to regard its Phoenix—like success over the last two decades as mainly an effective symbolism of the progression of Killarney as a tourist centre. The success of the

by Patricia O'Reilly

O'Donoghue steered towards Irish business, dropped the cabaret to promote the best Irish acts available. So expansion continued at the Gleneagle, despite a country-wide recession.

1975 saw Maurice O'Donoghue's big break into the entertainment scene with the launching of John McNally in cabaret five nights a week for twelve weeks;

in 1976 he built his cabaret around Danny Doyle; '77 Dermot O'Brien and '78 Joe Cuddy. For the '79 season Cathal Dunne was the prime feature, together with the Furey Brothers, Davey Arthur, Johnny McEvoy, Dermot O'Brien, Joe Loss, Joe Dolan, etc — the budget for entertainment for this year is £130,000. This figure does not allow for promotion, maintenance or salary costs. Over simplifying the matter, O'Donoghue explains, "The new professionalism amongst Irish entertainers made all this possible". The Gleneagle Country Club, Entertainment and sporting facilities cater for 250,000 patrons a year. The Club includes a ballroom, which multi-purposes for cabaret, dancing, socials and weddings, a large singing pub — the Eagle's Nest — used for disco, weddings, socials, pub theatre, etc. There are two squash courts, two hard court tennis courts, an 18 hole per 3 golf course, an 18 hole pitch and putt course, two snooker tables, children's games and extensive car parking space. The whole complex is sited in thirty acres south of Killarney.

Worrying his pipe, which he uses as a constant prop, O'Donoghue is relatively self conscious about his image locally. He mutters about "scotching the idea of being totally mercenary". He is not. The fact that fiscally he is very viable owes much to being in the right place at the right time and having the acumen to back his hunch to the hilt. His attitude to success is ambivalent — he is a pharmacist by duty — "I qualified because I had to — I was the eldest son in a family of seven and if anything had happened to my father we couldn't have afforded to employ a pharmacist, so I would have had to have been able to take over"; and an entertainment entrepreneur by inclination, "When you are directly involved with the customer it is most important that you be concerned with customer satisfaction. It is as important as making money. If you don't do it, you won't make money for very long". Along the route of his particular choosing he has amassed a personal fortune — in an incidental sort of way.

His cynicism and chauvinism interlink and are gentle without long term malice — taking the form of quick stabs at today's society and its petty pretensions; decrying nuns' newfound liberation, snide slaps at politicans; past running battles with Bord Failte and

The O'Donoghue Family, from left to right (back) Maurice, John, Margaret and Padraic and (front) Aine, Maurice and Stella.

tongue-in-cheek jeering of women's lib.

Talking about his children's future, he would like them to base their lifestyle on a commercial, rather than professional basis, which allows "better independence and scope for personal expression". Ideally he would look for individual analysis, so that each's full potential could be realised; would never point them in the direction of the Gleneagle (but the two eldest spent their summerholidays working in the Clubhouse) and would prefer that the money they receive be unrelated to work. Indeed his own early memories of initmate association with the daily business of a chemist's shop may have much to do with his attitude towards his children. He draws definite parallels between the functioning of a chemists and a hotel; but feels he owes much to his parent's foresight and outlook in giving him a business education — "As well as the diligence, perfection and ethics of pharmacy, it is a very factual profession, where you can't take shortcuts and we were brought

up with the idea of serving the public and all this has contributed to the success of the Gleneagle."

Following in the family tradition Maurice O'Donoghue has a republican outlook and he joined the Fianna Fail party in the mid '60s; in 1967 he headed the Fianna Fail poll in the election for the Killarney Urban District Council, was chairman in 1969 and re-elected in 1974 and 1979. Of his commitment to this he explains, "I am more interested in the UDC than in involvement in any other area of politics because I have deep concern for Killarney and where it's going. Being a member of the Urban Council gives you a standing, provides you with a platform and gives you a voice, but unfortunately local authorities have very little power." In full stride and obvious control of a pet hobby-horse, O'Donoghue feels there is too much power centered in Dublin; that there should be a major re-organisation of the geographic areas covered by the local authorities, and he cites Killarney, "Most of the lake district is outside the

jurisdiction of the Urban Council, but the most depressing and annoying thing is that other statutory authorities feel that matters they are undertaking in Killarney are of no concern to the UDC and often the Council is not even consulted — the Killarney Estate, bordering Killarney town to the south and west bought by the Office of Public works in conjunction with Bord Failte and the Kerry County Council and the last body to know anything about it, or have any say in it, was the Killarney Urban District Council. "Indeed, " he finishes with a characteristic toss of the head, "it is lack of authority, not interest that has prevented the Council doing more — even the main road running through Killarney isn't our responsibility".

But with all that success under his belt, O'Donoghue is not proposing to rest on his laurels. Within the immediate future he plans to start the Gleneagle Brass and Reed Band, "incorporating a school of music for brass and reed instruments". He will sponsor a full time teacher in Killarney, because as he explains it is entertainment and music that have put Gleneagle on the map and his motives are not purely philanthropic either. Firstly such a foundation would be good promotion; put back sponsorship and fulfil a need for the youth. Also he would like to get involved in employing a group in, say, a small manufacturing industry.

The Kerry slur and the manana voice are at odd variance with Maurice O'Donoghue's achievements. He has a reticence about personal divulgement — admits he never goes out for meals, talks about "food fatigue", which he deems inescapable in a hotel or restaurant, likes to eat Irish Stew with the children; drinks in moderation on an on/off basis; finds the study of Irish characteristics and business methods fascinating; feels a lot of the success in Ireland is due to people who have a faith and pride in what they do. "Most Irish people have an inferiority complex — I have one myself, but the more I study Irish people, their history, culture and music, the prouder I become".

But what makes Maurice O'Donoghue succeed where thousands of others would fail? It has to be a blend of heritage and personal chemistry, mixed with the basic instinct of the veteran gambler.

- The tourism and construction industry in Killarney is in for a boomtime.
- The hotels in the country's tourism capital have embarked on a massive development programme.
- Over the winter months £4 million will be spent on extensions and refurbishment.
- Tim Vaughan reports.

Tourism and building boom worth £4m

Killarney hotelier Maurice O'Donoghue is spending £2m. on two of his hotels.

WE hear reports from various parts of the country that it has been another bad tourist season. Bord Failte tells us the figures are up, and the PDs say the Bord's figures are wrong. And Government Ministers like to mention that tourism is a growth area.

Words, as the saying goes, are cheap — a lot cheaper than hotel bedrooms or bathrooms or diningrooms. Over the coming winter months, a small group of Killarney hoteliers will put their pockets where Ministers put their mouths and state their faith in the industry with investments of over £4 million.

The biggest building programme for years in Killarney hotel business has already got underway and involves all grades, from the 'A star' Hotel Europe to the family-run Grade 'C' Belvedere. By next spring, most of the work — which has come as a tremendous boom to the local building industry — will be complete and financed without State assistance. The huge investment — involving everything from building sports halls to refurbishing bedrooms —

> "By next spring most of the work — which has come as a tremendous boom to the local building industry — will be completed and financed without State assistance."

comes at the end of a season which most of the hoteliers involved agree was a good one. "It was slow to start but picked up very well and ran on late," was how one hotelier described the season — a view shared by a local tourism official.

The sharp fall in the number of visitors from the US was compensated

by an increase in those from continental Europe and Australia. But the developments now taking place have been planned for some time, and have more to do with optimism about the future than anything else.

The news that foreign tourists would be flying directly into Farranfore next year has increased the hoteliers' optimism, but, there again, they had made their decisions long before that announcement.

The biggest investment is being made by the GlenEagle Hotel: a £1½ million indoor sports complex which will include a 25-metre swimming pool and possibly a bowling alley.

Work is due to begin on the complex early in the new year and when completed will make the hotel one of the best in the country for leisure facilities. The sports hall will also have tennis and basketball courts, and the hotel already caters for a number of sports.

The GlenEagle's owner, Maurice O'Donoghue, is spending a further £500,000 on the refurbishment of his other hotel, Scott's, and the addition of another 12 bedrooms to the GlenEagle. The work on Scott's has already started and the remainder will begin in January.

So far this year his "Destination Killarney" marketing drive has brought

40,000 people to the town, and a fortnight ago a party of 250 Americans came for a four day trip, a pilot scheme based along the lines of the hugely successful "Showtime Express."

Two Killarney hotels are in the process of significantly increasing their bedroom capacity, the grade A Castlerosse is adding on an extra 25, plus a new reception area, a mini-gym and a sauna — at a cost of approximately £500,000. This should also create an extra four or five jobs during peak season, said manager Joe Leonard.

Work has also started on the construction of an additional 22 bedrooms at the grade 'B Star' family-run Royal Hotel, giving owners Joe and Margaret Scally a total of 50 rooms. They are also carrying

> "The Destination Killarney marketing drive has brought 40,000 people to the town."

out a refurbishment of the bar and restaurant and are putting in an elevator — at a total minimum cost of £400,000.

Liebherr International, owners of the Hotel Europe and Dunloe Castle, are at present building an indoor tennis hall, with two courts at each hotel, costing between three and four hundred thousand pounds in total. "We are conscious of the need to provide our guests with all weather facilities — and this is in keeping with the Price Waterhouse report," said general manager Ruth Grosjean.

Another family-run hotel, the Ross, has begun an off-season upgrading of its facilities. Its dining room, lounge area and 15 bedrooms are being totally refurbished and next March three single story apartments will be a added to the four already owned by the hotel. Total cost: £200,000.

By next spring, the Three Lakes hotel will have each of its 70 bedrooms refurbished, at a cost of £200,000 and the Lake Hotel is spending another £100,000 on refurbishment — on top of a similar ammount last year.

The owner of the Belvedere, John Lyne, says he has "great faith in the town's future" and is backing up his words with £60,000 for work on his hotel, which will transform it from a "three months of year operation" to an all-year round business. "And that will mean more jobs too, of course," he said.

200 construction jobs this winter

Ted Fitzgerald.

THE large amount of investment in the Killarney hotel industry this winter has come as a godsend to the building industry.

It's very welcome indeed — there hasn't been so much activity in the building industry in Killarney for a long time," said Ted Fitzgerald, President of the Construction Federation of Ireland.

It was also been welcomed by chairman of the Kerry branch of the CFI, John King, who is the owner of the Three Lakes Hotel.

"It's the first winter in a few years in Killarney that so much building is going on," he said. He estimated that up to 200 jobs could be involved in all.

In addition to the hotel building projects, work has also started on the £¾ million extension and refurbishment of the golf clubhouse and the £280,000 alterations to Fitzgerald stadium.

The construction of the £1 million-plus offices for the decentralisation of the Department of Justice is also expected to begin in early 1989.

Hotels spending the money

- GlenEagle — £1.5m sports complex.
- Scotts — £½m refurbishment.
- Castlerosse — £½m on 25 bedrooms and mini-gym.
- Royal Hotel — £400,000 on 22 bedrooms and refurbishment of bar and restaurant.
- Hotel Europe — £200,000 indoor tennis hall.
- Dunloe Castle — £200,000 indoor tennis hall.
- Ross Hotel — £200,000 on general refurbishment and new apartments.
- Three Lakes — £200,000 refurbishing bedrooms.
- The Lake Hotel — £100,000 on refurbishment.
- Belvedere — £60,000 upgrading.

The Kerryman, 25 November 1988.

In 1978 the couple purchased Scotts Hotel in Killarney's town centre. They immediately began making their mark on the property and over the years greatly extended the hotel. The iconic dome pictured here was built in 1988. (© Don MacMonagle, macmonagle.com)

Maurice and Margaret also focused on extending the traditional tourist season by introducing innovative package-holidays. Pictured here are patrons of The Showtime Express, filling The Gleneagle Hotel in early spring 1989.

The Showtime Express, devised and implemented by Maurice and Margaret O'Donoghue, was a resounding success and its benefits were felt throughout the town. The average train carried 500 passengers, a quarter of which opted to stay in The Gleneagle, the rest in hotels and guesthouses all over Killarney. Over 90 per cent of its passengers had never been to Killarney before. Entertainment was a huge draw with many of Ireland's top artists, including Christy Moore, Joe Cuddy, Dickie Rock, The Dubliners, Brendan Grace, The Fureys and Brendan Shine, taking to the stage of The Gleneagle Ballroom. The Sunday Morning Jazz Session in Scotts Hotel brought the weekends' festivities to a close. This picture was taken before the iconic dome was built. (© Don MacMonagle, macmonagle.com)

In May 1987 the hugely popular Showtime Express chugged its way directly from Heuston Station Dublin to Killarney for the very first time. In the years that followed over 20,000 Dubs boarded the party train and for just £49 bought into a revolutionary package – the first of its kind in Ireland. It included return train fare, two nights accommodation in one of Killarney's many hotels, nightly cabaret in The Gleneagle Ballroom and the famous Sunday Morning Jazz Session in Scotts Hotel.

(© Don MacMonagle, macmonagle.com)

Showtime Express to keep rolling

MAURICE O'Donoghue's Showtime Express, which has brought 1,500 people from Dublin to Killarney over the last three weekends, has been so successful that it is to be repeated in June/July.

A special train has brought 500 to the town each weekend, with a quarter of them staying at the GlenEagle Hotel and the remainder in other hotels in the town.

The visitors got two nights bed and breakfast and two nights of entertainment for £39.

The price will go up to £45 for the coming series of Showtime Express and artists booked for the Saturday night concerts include Dana, The Fureys, Brendan Shine and Christy Moore.

Every time the Express arrives in Killarney the GlenEgale band — and the chairman of the UDC, Sean O'Keeffe — are there to greet it. And there are flowers for all the ladies.

Maurice O'Donoghue said this week: "We're doing our bit to help Dublin to discover Ireland$"

The Kerryman,
22 May 1987.

Showtime Expres

Tony Kenny —one of the main attractions at the Showtime Express in the Gleneagle.

Another season of the highly successful Showtime Express got underway at the Gleneagle Hotel, Killarney, over the weekend when jazz musician Paddy Cole entertained the first of the revellers who arrived from Dublin.

now in its fifth year, it is estimated that the Express will bring an extra 3,500 visitors to Killarney over the autumn and winter — generating £½ million for the town.

The first Showtime Express arrived on Friday with 400 people on board. Coming to Killarney mainly for the cabaret and dancing, they were also offered sight-seeing tours, lake cruises, and local

The Express w extra 3,500 v Killarney and £½m for th

hospitality.

Another seve Express trains w town on Septemb ber 4, 11, 18, No 15 and 29.

The success of is rooted in a fo has now evolved trons two nigh breakfast, two n entertainment at gle Hotel, Sund jazz at Scotts Ga

The Kerryman, 4 October 1991.

In 1987 Maurice O'Donoghue teamed up with vintage-car collector Denis Lucey to open The Museum of Irish Transport. The museum housed a large collection of vintage cars, motorcycles and transport memorabilia. The jewel in the crown was undoubtedly the unique 1907 Silver Stream pictured here. (© Don MacMonagle, macmonagle.com)

ulls into town

candlelight dinner offered on selected departures. Prices range from £60 for guest-house accommodation to £75 for hotel accommodation.

Among the top Irish cabaret artistes who will be entertaining at the Gleneagle Hotel for the Showtime Express over the coming weeks will be Tony Kenny, Red Hurley, Dickie Rock, Johnny McEvoy, Joe Cuddy and the Dublin City Ramblers.

Another attraction at the Gleneagle Hotel is the very popular Dancing for Pleasure on Sunday nights. Admission per couple is £5 with the dance music continuing from 10.30pm to 12.30am.

Johnny Mc Evoy—one of the star attractions at the Showtime Express in the Gleneagle.

Maurice O'Donoghue's plan to introduce a waterbus to the Lakes of Killarney initially met with controversy, as it was the first of its kind in Ireland. The covered, heated vessel was intended to make the lakes more accessible to Killarney's visitors and is still in operation today.

(© Don MacMonagle, macmonagle.com)

May 5 1991   THE SUNDAY BUSINESS POST   A11

May 5 '91 (handwritten)

NEWS

James Morrissey speaks to Killarney hotelier Maurice O'Donoghue whose expansion programme is being backed by rivals

Hotelier defies BES setback to grow and grow again

JERRY KENNELLY / NEWSPAX

Maurice O'Donoghue: "We never thought the showband era would last 30 years. The investment we made came from the dance hall"

"The knocker will tell you that Killarney is over-commercialised. What he means by that is that you can buy whatever you want in Killarney," says hotelier Maurice O'Donoghue.

Over 30 years O'Donoghue has emerged a dynamic entrepreneur in the hotel and entertainment industries and is currently undertaking a £10 million expansion programme at the GlenEagle hotel, on the outskirts of Killarney.

The programme began last year with a 48-bedroom extension and is being continued this year with another 44 bedrooms and a leisure centre. Planning permission has been granted for a further 80 bedrooms, rooftop garden restaurants and a conference hall. The owner wants to have 250 bedrooms eventually.

O'Donoghue is constantly assessing new ideas, new projects and innovative holiday packages to develop the GlenEagle into a 10-month business. "In the last three or four years we've been quite busy from the beginning of March up to and including December. January and February are our only slack months really. We are always very busy at weekends but there have been some gaps mid-week. Some time ago we ran a ballroom dancing competition mid-week and we had

200 people. You'll find that if you're a good listener the ideas will come."

Maurice O'Donoghue went to Dublin in the mid-1950s to study pharmacy. While there he frequented many of the city's dance halls. "I liked the idea of running dances. In 1959 I ran the first dance here in Killarney, it was the beginning of the showband boom." That dance was held in the large function room in the Victorian house which his parents has acquired.

"I qualified as a pharmacist but I never practised. My father was a very active man. We had a chemist's shop in the town and it wasn't big enough for the two of us."

The showband era was good to O'Donoghue. "We never thought it would last 30 years. The investment we made basically came from the box office in the dance hall." Today the GlenEagle is a 90,000 square feet hotel and entertainment centre. During a recent weekend a Dublin group played bingo at breakfast as part of a packaged weekend during which a wide range of activities were on offer.

The GlenEagle employs 120 people full-time. "Because of the nature of the business it is a seven-day week, 15-hour day. You know you have to have three receptionists to do one job." Turnover last year exceeded £3 million.

O'Donoghue places great emphasis on marketing and operates an office in Dublin together with a counter in Clerys store on O'Connell Street. He

has seven people working in sales and marketing. Monitoring trends and visitor numbers is something O'Donoghue is diligent about. Last

year 54 per cent of his visitors were Irish, 23 per cent from the UK, 13 per cent from the United States and 10 per cent from mainland Europe.

Four years ago O'Donoghue set up Destination Killarney, a handling agency. Since 1987 the company has handled educational tours in the area for over 17,000 young people and has booked over 200,000 bed-nights into all grades of accommodation in Killarney. The company organised Showtime Express, a weekend entertainment package offered in conjunction with Irish Rail which resulted in 20,000 Dubliners travelling to Killarney, using 20 hotels. It has been estimated that 90 per cent of those who travelled on the Showtime Express train had never been to Killarney and the same percentage

"We are keenly aware that there are certain things that we have to do together – including the upgrading and protection of the environment," O'Donoghue has said

had not been on a train for 10 years.

Destination Killarney has been given the task of arranging 1,500 beds for 15 nights for the European Bridge Congress which takes place next month. Also coming up is the Carrolls Irish Open.

To coincide with the golf spectacular, the GlenEagle has assembled a series of packaged breaks which include meals, accommodation, tickets for the golf and nightly cabaret.

Last year was a traumatic one for O'Donoghue. Just when he thought he had organised BES funding for extra bedrooms he was taken ill and spent some time in hospital. "When I

came out of hospital the Dublin company which was organising the funds told us there was no BES funding. We were let down badly."

Immediately O'Donoghue set about raising £600,000 locally in Killarney which he did without difficulty. "A lot of our investors are local and, funnily enough, some of our investors are other hoteliers." The reason for this is that Destination Killarney has benefited many local businesses, including competing hotels. O'Donoghue's belief is that Killarney's success as a tourism centre is, due, to a great extent, to people working together.

"All businesses in Killarney aim to maximise their own potential. Killarney is the most competitive and best-value tourist destination in Ireland. But yet we are also keenly aware that there are certain things that we have to do together – the upgrading and protection of the environment, making sure that appropriate development strategies are undertaken by local authorities and central government," O'Donoghue said at the official opening of the new bedroom block last year.

Today the GlenEagle has seven self-contained entertainment centres capable of offering seven different forms of entertainment catering for up to 4,000 people at one time.

The water leisure centre which is under construction will be in operation by August. Costing £1.5 million, it will include a 25-metre swimming pool, water slides, sauna and steam rooms, gym and therapy room. Ancillary facilities will include squash and tennis courts, pitch and putt and bowling.

O'Donoghue's other business interests in Killarney include Killarney Waterbus, Scotts Hotel and a transport museum.

However, his main focus is the development of the GlenEagle which is being assisted with £1 million of BES funding this year. "When we've this plan completed, sure, we might look at something else. You'd never know."

Sunday Business Post, 5 May 1991.

In 1987 the O'Donoghues founded Destination Killarney. Its purpose was to market Killarney and its many attractions both at home and abroad. Destination Killarney had offices in Killarney, Dublin and London. The Destination Killarney Kiosk, located on East Avenue Road, acted as an information desk and booking office for Killarney's growing number of visitors.

(© Don MacMonagle, macmonagle.com)

Killarney group plans to spend £1m to attract more tourists

A MARKETING organisation which has sold over 250,000 bednights in Killarney over the past six years is to expand its operations into Britain with a marketing budget of £1m and the opening of an office in London.

Destination Killarney was set up as the marketing arm of the Gleneagle Hotel and Scotts Hotel in Killarney — owned by local businessman and Town Council Chairman Maurice O'Donoghue.

Concentrating on selling holidays in Killarney on the Irish market, it expanded quickly to market other hotels and guesthouses throughout the town also. The Showtime Express weekend breaks in conjunction with Irish Rail has been its most identifiable success.

Now Destination Killarney is to expand its operations into Britain, with the announcement this week that £1m is to be raised to spearhead a marketing drive there. Destination Killarney has been sanctioned for a £500,000 Business Expansion Scheme and has already raised £350,000 from the corporate sector through this scheme.

A drive to raise another £150,000 from the tourism industry in Kerry will begin shortly and the organisation's backers are aiming to raise the remaining £500,000 through the European Regional Development Fund.

While it has not been guaranteed ERDF assistance, Destination Killarney says the fund is to be extended to include marketing projects and it is confident of qualifying on the basis of its track record.

Destination Killarney has already opened an office in London which is being headed up by a former contracts manager with Gullivers Travel, Pat Murphy. A feasibility study is currently being carried out and Mr Murphy is exploring niche markets which Destination Killar-

By Paschal Sheehy

ney could tap into, such as golf, hill-walking and other activity holidays. Also, as the company expands in Britain, a greater emphasis will be placed on selling Kerry as a destination rather than Killarney on its own.

Destination Killarney Chairman Maurice O'Donoghue said this week that if tourism is to be expanded in Kerry more money will have to be spent on marketing. He said he felt that specific groups doing their own marketing was more desireable than a single marketing campaign co-ordinated through all tourism interests in the county.

"I think going after niche markets is the way to go after business. Other people might have different views. I am not totally in favour of putting geographical barriers on what you are marketing because people in England don't necessarily distinguish between Kerry and Cork and Killarney and Glengarriff," he said.

He said marketing was "a necessity" and the expansion of Destination was particularly appropriate given that Kerry Airport's new facilities will be operational for this year's tourist season.

"The development of Kerry Airport is extremely important. However, I don't think we can expect the airport itself to do all the marketing for the county. There will have to be structures like Destination Killarney developed to use the airport to market the county and its amenities," Mr O'Donoghue said.

He said the initial response to Destination Killarney's expansion into Britain was positive but added: "One has to be realistic about marketing. It is something from which you may not get a response for 12 months."

The Kerryman, 14 January 1994.

WEEKEND February 1, 1992 Page 13

LEADING KERRY HOTELIER'S PLEA FOR CABLE CARS AND A TOUCH OF LAS VEGAS FOR KILLARNEY

THE THOUGHT of cable-cars criss-crossing the mountains of Killarney, not to mention the opening of late-night gambling casinos, is enough to make some environmentalists and moralists cringe — but not everybody in "Heaven's Reflex" thinks that way.

One of the area's leading hoteliers, Maurice O'Donoghue, believes for instance that cable-cars — ruled out completely by the Office of Public Works, the body responsible for managing the area's 25,000-acre national park — should again be considered.

"The sights should be made accessible to as many people as possible. It's fine for people who're well able to climb up Mangerton, for example, and enjoy the glorious views from the top but those who cannot go up there because of age or disability should also be facilitated," declared the first man to put a controversial waterbus on the lakes.

Under-utilised

"Everybody agrees that our amenities are completely under-utilised and anything that can be done to develop them correctly should be encouraged."

And neither would the tourism entrepreneur with a yen for Alpine transport see anything wrong with bringing a touch of Las Vegas, in the form of licensed casinos, to his hometown. "Tourists expect such facilities in all leading resorts around the world," he remarked.

But, there are more serious and mundane matters to be dealt with first. Now extending a traditional one million visitors annually, Killarney may soon be unable to cope with the influx.

"We're not short of bedrooms or entertainment for tourists but something needs to be done urgently to help relieve traffic congestion and to improve infrastructural services. But, there's no co-ordinated plan to cater for the obvious growth that's taking place," maintained Mr. O'Donoghue, in an interview with the "Weekender."

In his view, Bord Failte, Kerry Co. Council and the OPW are working to their own briefs but they should get together to formulate an overall plan for the future of the country's leading resort.

Relief road

As he sees it, the provision of a relief road from the Muckross side of the town to the Killorglin side is an absolute "must" so as to take traffic from choked town centre in peak season. Problem now is that most visitors have to go through the town to reach the most popular beauty spots.

Indeed, he feels, the town centre should ultimately be pedestrianised; footpaths widened and no car parking allowed. But that could not be done until adequate off-street car parks were laid on. The centrally-located Glebe property, which the Town Council has been talking about purchasing for countless years, should also be acquired.

"With the present congestion, visitors are being discouraged from going into the middle of town but we must bring about a situation where they'll find it easy to stroll around and do their shopping in comfort. I've no doubt that traders would also do much better if that was the situation," he opined.

Other features to enhance the appearance of the town would include a permanent, decorative lighting system;

STORY: DONAL HICKEY

Maurice O'Donoghue, prominent Killarney hotelier.

PICTURE: DENIS SCANNELL

the floodlighting of all buildings of architectural importance and the construction of a fountain.

In his own business at the Gleneagle Hotel, Mr. O'Donoghue has proved to be innovative and responsive to public demands. His latest venture is an ultra-modern swimming pool/leisure centre — the biggest of its kind in any hotel in Ireland — and he's currently planning a 2,500-seat conference/concert centre.

The hotel, which had eleven bedrooms when brought by the O'Donoghue family in 1957, now has 180 as well extensive facilities for entertainment. Unlike many places in Killarney, up to 50% of the hotel's business is Irish.

Mr. O'Donoghue believes that it will take the US market another three or four years to recover but ever-increasing numbers of European visitors should compen-sate. Continentals tend to favour outdoor, activity holidays but, are services geared to cater for their needs?

Golf continues to soar in popularity but, here again, Killarney's existing two championship courses are hard-pressed to cope. He sees no reason why the OFW should not make some of its 25,000 acres available for additional golf facilities and said that he and other hoteliers would only be too happy to financially support such ventures.

Always thinking ahead, he strongly argues for the improvement of roads, rail, water and sewerage services.

"I can see a road from Killarney to Kenmare in 50 years time going around the other side of the mountains with the existing road through Lady's View and Moll's Gap being kept strictly as a tourist, scenic route," he predicted.

Maurice's predictions for Killarney's future, *The Examiner*, 1 February 1992.

In 1967, Maurice O'Donoghue was elected to Killarney UDC. He held the seat until his death in 2001 and was elected chairman of the council on three occasions. Upon his death, the UDC chairman, Cllr Sean Counihan, described Maurice as a visionary whose overriding priority was always Killarney. 'He was the difference between home and emigration for quite a lot of people', *Irish Examiner*, 12 June 2001. (© Don MacMonagle, macmonagle.com)

The Gleneagle Band

The Killarney Brass and Reed Band had entertained the people of Killarney before they disbanded in the 1950s. Maurice O'Donoghue believed that the town should, once again, have its own band, always at the ready for public functions and occasions, and so began his sponsorship of The Gleneagle Concert Band and School of Music. (© Don MacMonagle, macmonagle.com)

The Gleneagle School of Music was established in 1980 with a view to it becoming a resource pool for band members and by the end of 1981 The Gleneagle Concert Band was ready to perform in public. Before long they were performing at parades, festivals and events not just in Killarney but all over Europe. (© Michelle Cooper-Galvin)

The Gleneagle Concert Band, 1987. All instruments in The Gleneagle School of Music are loaned to members free of charge. This way, students have the opportunity to try out an instrument without having to make a huge monetary investment. While The Gleneagle Hotel has remained the main sponsor of the band throughout the years, there have been many generous donations from other businesses and individuals, including Joe Dolan who donated a number of instruments when the band was first established. (© Don MacMonagle, macmonagle.com)

The Gleneagle Concert Band performs for Taoiseach Charles Haughey in 1987.

The Gleneagle Concert Band performs at The Market Cross in Killarney as part of the St Patrick's Day celebrations in 2003.

Gleneagle Concert Band member Kate Curran hitting the right notes in the Killarney Summerfest Community Parade in July 2006. (© Valerie O'Sullivan)

Conductor Vincent Condon giving instruction to The Gleneagle Concert Band as they perform a free concert on the streets of Killarney in 2012. (© Valerie O'Sullivan)

Band member Peter O'Donoghue, grandson of Maurice O'Donoghue, performs with The Gleneagle Concert Band. The School of Music's Education Youth Programme offers tuition on clarinet, flute, saxophone, trumpet, French horn, trombone, euphonium, tuba, drums and singing. The band is renowned for excellence and provides a first-class, comprehensive and complete programme including one-to-one instrumental lessons, theory classes and various ensemble groups. All band staff are internationally renowned, professionally qualified teachers with extensive performance and teaching experience. (© Valerie O'Sullivan)

The Gleneagle Concert Band performs at a charity concert at The Gleneagle Hotel in March 2015. (© Nerijus Karmilcovas)

The O'Donoghue Clan

Organising festivals has been an O'Donoghue tradition since before The Gleneagle was even established. In 1954 Paddy O'Donoghue played a key role in coordinating the O'Donoghue Clan Rally and Pageant. Over 2,000 people, from Ireland, Britain and the US, converged on Killarney for this festival, which celebrated the O'Donoghue Clan's cultural and historic ties to the town. (© Harry MacMonagle, macmonagle.com)

Trumpets sounded a call from the ramparts of Ross Castle to open the ceremony that took place on the green below. A colourful parade of the Chieftain's entourage, dressed in period costumes, marched to the castle through a guard of honour of O'Donoghue clansmen. Geoffrey O'Donoghue, the O'Donoghue of the glen and central figure of the pageant, was seated on the Leac Na Rioghthigh stone, specially brought from Killaha Castle at Glenflesk, and inaugurated as Chieftain of the Clan. (© Harry MacMonagle, macmonagle.com)

The Gathering

Musician Henry Cronin launches The Gathering Traditional Festival in 2009. With a finely tuned mix of concerts, *céilís*, workshops and sessions, The Gathering has been the highlight of the Irish cultural calendar for traditional musicians and *céilí* dancers alike since its inception back in 1999. This festival takes place every February at The Gleneagle Hotel. (© Valerie O'Sullivan)

Master Craftsman Tim O'Carroll working on one of his Killarney Harps ahead of The Gathering Traditional Festival in The Gleneagle Hotel in 2014. He is one of only a handful of skilled craftsmen in Ireland making harps today. (© Valerie O'Sullivan)

Renowned storyteller Eddie Lenihan, recounting stories of myth, mystery and folklore at The Gathering Traditional Festival at The Gleneagle Hotel in 2014.
(© Valerie O'Sullivan)

Devoted set dancers dancing the Sliabh Luachra set at The Gathering Traditional Festival's *Céilí Mór* in The Gleneagle Hotel in 2007. (© Valerie O'Sullivan)

Crowds gather for the *Céilí Mór* at The Gathering Traditional Irish Festival in 2013. (© Valerie O'Sullivan)

Faye O'Donoghue and Jennifer Rea, having their own fun at The Gathering Traditional Festival in February 2015.

(© Valerie O'Sullivan)

Ciara O'Shea, dancing with musicians from The Killarney School of Music, watched adoringly by Ava Power, at The Gathering Traditional Festival in 2012. (© Valerie O'Sullivan)

Paudie O'Connor, Matt Cranitch and Jackie Daly enjoying an impromptu session at The Gathering Traditional Festival in 2014. (© Valerie O'Sullivan)

Feithleann Somers playing a Killarney Harp at The Gathering Traditional Festival in 2014. (© Valerie O'Sullivan)

Derrick Ahare enjoying the fiddle workshop at The Gathering Traditional Festival in 2005. (© Valerie O'Sullivan)

Mairead Casey giving a *Séan Nós* dancing workshop at The Gathering Traditional Festival. (© Valerie O'Sullivan)

The Schools Outreach Programme is one of the most popular elements of The Gathering Festival. Every year a group of musicians and dancers visit primary schools in the Killarney area. The students and teachers are treated to a feast of toe-tapping tunes and are given a unique insight into their culture and heritage in a fun and interactive way. Here pupils from Fossa National School, Killarney, enjoy a music demonstration by piper Padraig Buckley. (© Valerie O'Sullivan)

Séan Nós at its best. Ciaran Quigley and Sean O'Shea, pupils at Loughquittane National School, Killarney stepping it out as part of the Schools Outreach Programme in 2009. (© Valerie O'Sullivan)

The Voice Squad with Gerry Cullen, Phil Callery and Fran McPhail performing *The Parting Glass* at The Gathering Traditional Festival in 2014. (© Valerie O'Sullivan)

Manus and Séamus McGuire, Garry O'Briain and Jackie Daly reunite as Buttons and Bows, for a concert at The Gathering Traditional Festival in 2014. (© Valerie O'Sullivan)

Cathy Jordan, lead singer with Dervish, performing at The Gathering Traditional Festival in 2013. (© Valerie O'Sullivan)

Orlaith and Brogan McAuliffe in concert with Tim O'Shea at The Gathering Traditional Festival in 2015.
(© Valerie O'Sullivan)

A light beams
over the late, great
Johnny O'Leary's
accordion at the
Johnny O'Leary
Tribute night in 2006.
(© Valerie O'Sullivan)

Summerfest

Professor Plunger and Festy the Clown with Zio Geaney and Ellen Greene, launching Killarney Summerfest 2011. This family-friendly festival attracted thousands of visitors from all around the world to Killarney with its jam-packed programme of concerts, theatre, street entertainment and workshops. (© Valerie O'Sullivan)

Paul from the Wobbly Circus entertaining festivalgoers at Killarney Summerfest 2009. (© Valerie O'Sullivan)

Toons – The Professional Idiot from Denmark, winner of
Killarney Summerfest's International Busking Competition
2006, who dazzled the crowd with his 3-metre-high
unicycle and giant balloon tricks. (© Valerie O'Sullivan)

Members of the Azar Teatro Troupe performing at Killarney Summerfest's International Busking Competition 2003. The highest calibre of street entertainers from around the world descended on Killarney to compete in the three-day competition, which was a highlight of the Summerfest programme. Thousands of spectators gazed in utter bewilderment at the bizarre and fantastic antics of the various contortionists, fire-eaters, jugglers and acrobats. (© Valerie O'Sullivan)

Taking chivalry to new heights. Paul from the Wobbly Circus shelters an unsuspecting lady on the streets of Killarney in 2009. (© Valerie O'Sullivan)

Top make-up tips at Killarney Summerfest 2010. (© Valerie O'Sullivan)

Don't try this at home! The Great Mefiesto flabbergasts kids at Killarney Summerfest 2010. (© Valerie O'Sullivan)

Spreading magic on the streets of Killarney. Maya of the Magic Street Theatre lights up the town during Summerfest 2011. (© Valerie O'Sullivan)

Buí Bolg Puppeteer
'Bríd from the Bar' doing
the rounds at Killarney
Summerfest 2011.
(© Valerie O'Sullivan)

A scene from *Merlin the Magician* performed by Chapterhouse Theatre
Company at Muckross House and Gardens in 2009. (© Valerie O'Sullivan)

Touring theatre company Chapterhouse perform *King Arthur and the Knights of the Round Table* on the spectacular grounds of Muckross House and Gardens for Killarney Summerfest 2008.

(© Valerie O'Sullivan)

Sharon Corr performing with Irish band The Corrs at Fitzgerald's Stadium in 2004. Killarney Summerfest attracted top international artists to perform at the festival's outdoor concerts.

(© Valerie O'Sullivan)

Meatloaf entertaining thousands of fans at a Killarney Summerfest concert at Fitzgerald's Stadium in 2005.

(© Valerie O'Sullivan)

Westlife perform to their
adoring fans at their
Killarney Summerfest
open-air concert in 2008.
(© Valerie O'Sullivan)

Nicole Scherzinger and the Pussycat Dolls light up the stage
at Killarney Summerfest 2009. (© Valerie O'Sullivan)

Rocking all over the world. Legendary rocker Francis Rossi of Status Quo entertaining thousands of fans at a Killarney Summerfest outdoor concert at Fitzgerald's Stadium in 2005.
(© Valerie O'Sullivan)

Pink performs at Killarney
Summerfest 2007.
(© Valerie O'Sullivan)

Elton John, Counting Crows,
Tom Jones, Bryan Adams and
David Gray were just some of
the many other international
artists who performed to capacity
crowds at Killarney Summerfest's
outdoor concerts at Fitzgerald's
Stadium. (© Valerie O'Sullivan)

If you go down to the woods today … families gather at Muckross House and Gardens for Killarney Summerfest's Teddy Bears' Picnic in 2012.

(© Valerie O'Sullivan)

Sharing her lollipop with her teddy.
Ellen McSweeney at Killarney
Summerfest's Teddy Bears' Picnic in 2008.
(© Valerie O'Sullivan)

Lily Kent shares her cupcake with her
teddies at Muckross House and Gardens
in 2009. (© Valerie O'Sullivan)

Ciara McClure at the Killarney Summerfest's Teddy Bears'
Picnic in 2012. (© Valerie O'Sullivan)

Up, up and away! Hot-air balloons rise over Killarney as part of Summerfest 2006. The three-day hot-air-balloon spectacle was a highlight of the festival programme. (© Valerie O'Sullivan)

Balloon operator Joe Healy checks his balloon before firing it up at Killarney Summerfest 2006. Twelve balloonists from the UK and Ireland descended upon the town for a weekend of flying. (© Valerie O'Sullivan)

As dusk approached neighbours and friends came out in force to help the balloon crew who landed close-by during Killarney Summerfest 2007. (© Valerie O'Sullivan)

On top of the world. A balloon rises above St Mary's Cathedral at Killarney Summerfest 2006. (© Valerie O'Sullivan)

Bikefest [there are 9 more pictures that could be used for this section if you want them]

In 2006, 5,000 HOG (Harley Davidson Owners Group) members first rumbled into Killarney for their annual rally and the town hasn't been the same since! The people of Killarney fell head over wheels in love with the biking community and so an annual biker festival, Ireland Bike Fest, was born. Ireland Bike Fest is now a well-oiled machine, attracting tens of thousands of bike enthusiasts from all over the world. Ireland's only free open biker festival, this motorcycle and music extravaganza takes place annually across the June Bank Holiday weekend. (© Eamonn Keogh, macmonagle.com)

Mountains and motorcycles. Ireland Bike Fest at The Gleneagle Hotel, 2009.

(© Valerie O'Sullivan)

Aspiring bikers Muiris O'Donoghue, Eoghan McSweeney and their dog Hugo getting up close to a Harley Davidson bike at the Ireland Bike Fest Village at The Gleneagle Hotel in 2009. (© Don MacMonagle, macmonagle.com)

Parked up at The Gleneagle Hotel, the official headquarters for the annual festival. All makes, models and manner of bikes are welcome at Ireland Bike Fest. (© Don MacMonagle, macmonagle.com)

The Bike Village is the main hub of activity during Ireland Bike Fest. Trader stands sell all sorts of special-ised biker ware including clothing, helmets, trinkets, gadgets, and gizmos. (© Don MacMonagle, macmonagle.com)

Festivalgoers enjoying some of the free live music at Ireland Bike Fest 2014. (© Don MacMonagle, macmonagle.com)

Harry stands guard
over his owner's bike at
Ireland Bike Fest, 2009.
(© Valerie O'Sullivan)

Revving up. Sean Bennett at Ireland Bike Fest, 2009. (© Valerie O'Sullivan)

Cruising, chrome and a cracking good sound system! Pictured at Ireland Bike Fest 2014. (© Don MacMonagle, macmonagle.com)

Ready for the road at Ireland Bike Fest 2014. (© Don MacMonagle, macmonagle.com)

Killarney biker Pat Teahan pictured with Col. Gaddafi's old 1962 Harley Davidson motorbike at Ireland Bike Fest 2011. The bike was brought out from Libya by English diplomats and subsequently sold to Harley enthusiasts, none of whom were aware of its history. Teahan uncovered the link to the notorious dictator after discovering the original paperwork in a compartment of the historic vehicle. (© Don MacMonagle, macmonagle.com)

Motorcyclists Nigel Villiers, Paul Lusty, David Jones and Daniel Lovis taking a spin on the Kenmare road over Moll's Gap at Ireland Bike Fest, 2010. (© Valerie O'Sullivan)

Lenny Byrnes, Harley Davidson enthusiast with Arwynn O'Donoghue at Ireland Bike Fest 2010.
(© Valerie O'Donoghue)

Big-hearted bikers taking part in the festival parade through Killarney town in aid of Muscular Dystrophy
Ireland. Ireland Bike Fest is a proud supporter of Muscular Dystrophy Ireland and raffles a Harley Davidson
to raise funds for the charity each year. (© Eamonn Keogh, macmonagle.com)

Soaking up the scenery at Killarney's world-famous Ladies View during Ireland Bike Fest 2011.

(© Don MacMonagle, macmonagle.com)

Queens of the road Fiona Carroll, Eilish Coffey and Patricia O'Donoghue enjoying a pit stop by Killarney's Lough Leane during Ireland Bike Fest 2014.

(© Don MacMonagle, macmonagle.com)

Snap-happy bikers taking part in the annual Ireland Bike Fest parade, 2014.

(© Don MacMonagle, macmonagle.com)

CHAPTER FOUR

Sports and Events

The Gleneagle Hotel has a long association with sporting events, both in a hosting capacity and as a direct sponsor. An enthusiastic admirer of the Kerry football team throughout his life, Paddy O'Donoghue became an official sponsor during the 1960s and this spirit of giving has been part of the hotel's ethos ever since. Down through the years, The Gleneagle Hotel has been the official sponsor of various local and regional teams such as Dr Crokes football team and the Gleneagle Lakers basketball team.

The Gleneagle Hotel's Aquila Club provides facilities for both amateurs and professionals in a wide range of sports, including squash, pitch and putt, tennis and swimming. The flexibility of Ireland's National Events Centre allows the hall to transform into a world-class arena that has hosted top-class competitions from bowls to Taekwondo while the hotel's unique location has seen it as the hub for various road events.

For many The Gleneagle is synonymous with going for gold. Athletes from all over the world have travelled to Killarney to compete at the highest level. Past sporting events include the World Indoor Tug-of-War Championships, the World Irish Dancing Championships and the Munster Table Tennis Championships.

Not alone has The Gleneagle Hotel played host to some of the greatest sports in the world, it has also welcomed many a sporting hero. Greats such as Denis Taylor, Stephen Roche and John Aldridge have passed through the hotel's doors, both as competitors and holiday guests.

GAA/Kerry Football

Paddy O'Donoghue with Kerry goalkeeper Paudie O'Mahony and team trainer Mick O'Dwyer in 1976. Paddy, a long-standing supporter, had just presented the team with a cheque for £250. (© Kevin Coleman)

Paddy O'Donoghue presenting a cheque for £500 to Mr Frank King, chairman of the Kerry Country Board following Kerry's All-Ireland win in 1979. The Gleneagle cheque was a contribution towards the expenses of the football team's celebratory trip to America in October of that year. Paddy had previously travelled with the Kerry team on their historic world tour in 1969. Also pictured are trainer Mick O'Dwyer, Kerry Captain Tim Kennelly and John Kelly of the Kerry County Board. (© Kevin Coleman)

Kerry football trainer Jackie Lyon and team selector Johnny Culloty with Paddy O'Donoghue and the Sam McGuire cup in the Gleneagle Hotel.

Former GAA President Sean Kelly chats with delegates at the Kerry County Board AGM in The Gleneagle Hotel in 2002. (© Don MacMonagle, macmonagle.com)

Stars from the 1975 Kerry All-Ireland winning team, celebrating their silver jubilee at a special banquet held in The Gleneagle Hotel. Pictured are Captain Mickey Ned O'Sullivan and Ger Power with Manager Mick O'Dwyer. (© Eamon Keogh, macmonagle.com)

Pat Spillane and John Egan at the silver jubilee banquet held in The Gleneagle Hotel.

(© Eamon Keogh, macmonagle.com)

Pictured at the launch of the sponsorship renewal between The Gleneagle Hotel and Dr Crokes GAA Club were, from left, Kieran O'Leary, Colm Cooper, Shane Doolan, Dáithi Casey, Fionn Fitzgerald, Eoin Brosnan, Mike Maloney and Johnny Buckley with Patrick O'Donoghue and Dr Crokes Chairman Ger O'Shea.
(© Eamon Keogh, macmonagle.com)

The Gleneagle Hotel continues its long-standing support of Kerry football through its sponsorship of the Killarney club Dr Crokes. Patrick O'Donoghue is pictured with GAA stars Colm Cooper and Eoin Brosnan. (© Eamon Keogh, macmonagle.com)

Minister for Arts, Sports and Tourism John O'Donoghue TD, with GAA President Sean Kelly at the National GAA Club forum at the INEC in November 2005. (© Eamon Keogh, macmonagle.com)

'The battle is now over – we return our swords to the scabbard.' Páidí Ó Sé arrives at a press conference to announce his resignation as manager of the Kerry team in October 2003. Pictured in The Gleneagle Hotel flanked by Patrick O'Donoghue, Liam Higgins and Tom Long. (© Don MacMonagle, macmonagle.com)

Peter McKenna, stadium director of Croke Park, and Paddy Muldoon, Coiste Bainistí, at The National GAA Club Forum at the INEC in 2005. (© Valerie O'Sullivan)

Basketball

Heralding the beginning of the golden era in Killarney basketball, The Gleneagle Hotel sponsored the town's St Vincent's basketball team in the 1980s. (© Don MacMonagle, macmonagle.com)

Tony Andre (6ft 7in) and Arnold Veasely (6ft 4in), the first two American basketball players to play for The Gleneagle Basketball Team, signing autographs for brothers Maurice and John O'Donoghue in September 1981. (© Michelle Cooper-Galvin)

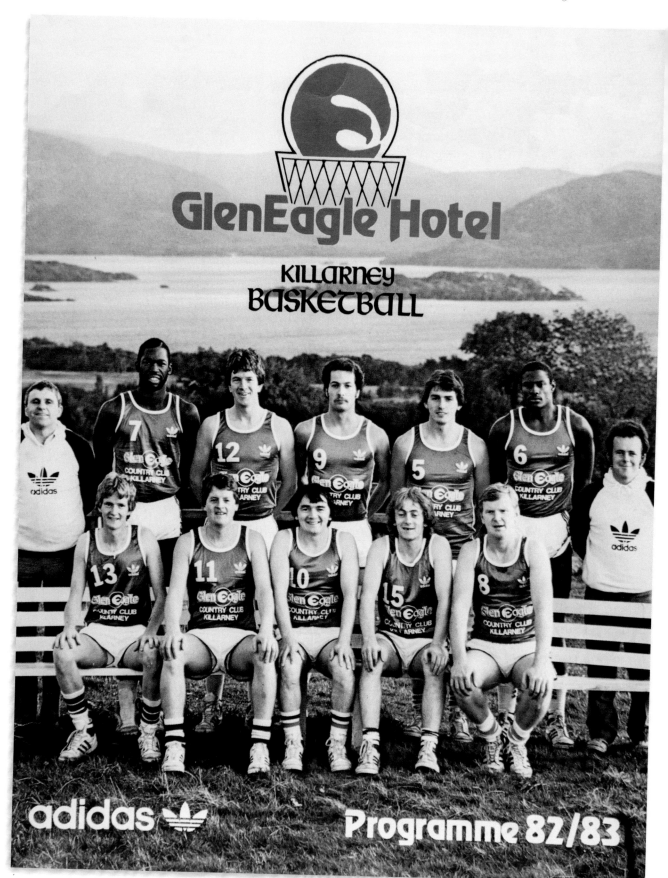

The Gleneagle Lakers play a home game at the newly
opened INEC in 2000. The maple floor of the INEC is
Irish Basketball Association approved.

(© Don MacMonagle, macmonagle.com)

Americans William Mayfield and
Maurice Carter sign with the Gleneagle
Lakers in October 2000. The Gleneagle
returned to the role of sponsors of
Killarney basketball from 2000 to 2007.

(© Eamonn Keogh, macmonagle.com)

The Gleneagle Hotel
Killarney Basketball
Programme 1982/83.

(© Don MacMonagle,

macmonagle.com)

Motorsport

The Gleneagle has been a mecca for motor enthusiasts since it first opened. Haulie Fitzpatrick, Maurice O'Donoghue and Paddy O'Donoghue test-drive a 1911 Rolls Royce that visited the hotel as part of a Vintage Rally in 1967. (© Kevin Coleman)

The Kerry Veteran and Vintage Classic Rally led by Maurice O'Donoghue driving his 1905 Argyll. This annual Vintage Rally is headquartered at The Gleneagle Hotel. (© Kevin Coleman)

Maurice O'Donoghue, Haulie
Fitzpatrick, Colm Foley, Niall
Fitzsimons and Padraig O'Donoghue
tour the Ring of Kerry in a 1905
Argyll as part of the Kerry Veteran
and Vintage Classic Rally 2001.
(© Eamonn Keogh, macmonagle.com)

The annual Rally of
the Lakes has been
headquartered at
The Gleneagle Hotel
since 1980. The stages
around Killarney are
justly renowned as some
of the finest tarmac
stages in Western Europe.
Millstreet Maestro Billy
Coleman dominated the
rally in the early years,
winning in 1979, 1983,
1984 and 1985. Billy is
pictured here with his
co-driver Ronan Morgan
and their Ford Escort G3
in 1985. (© Don MacMonagle,
macmonagle.com)

Austin McHale is interviewed by RTÉ's Vere Wynne-Jones having just won the 1986 Rally of the Lakes in his Opel Mantra 400. (© Don MacMonagle, macmonagle.com)

Dynamic duo Bertie Fisher and Rory Kennedy have won the Rally of the Lakes six times, a record that remains unbroken. (© Don MacMonagle, macmonagle.com)

In 1994 Killarney's Rally of the Lakes was granted European Championship status. Further flair was added with the entry of Tour de France winner Stephen Roche in a Ford Escort Cosworth. Pictured are Mike Marshall, clerk of the course, Stephen Roche and Patrick O'Donoghue. (© Don MacMonagle, macmonagle.com)

Andrew Nesbitt and James O'Brien celebrate on the bonnet of their Subaru after winning the Killarney Rally of the Lakes 2005.
(© Eamonn Keogh, macmonagle.com)

Snooker

The Gleneagle Hotel has a long association with the game of snooker. It hosts both the Munster and All-Ireland Snooker Championships annually and has welcomed many of the snooker greats down through the years.
(© Don MacMonagle, macmonagle.com)

World snooker champion Dennis Taylor holidays at The Gleneagle Hotel having just won the 1985 World Championship. Taylor beat world number one Steve Davis on the final black in one of the sport's most memorable finals. (© Don MacMonagle, macmonagle.com)

What a shootout! Some of the world's top snooker players lined up in a shootout at the INEC for the inaugural Liam O'Connor Memorial Snooker Championship in 2002. Pictured, from left to right, are: Ronnie O'Sullivan, Mark King, Fergal O'Brien, Paul Hunter, Tony Drago, Matthew Stephens, Ken Doherty and Nigel Bond. (© Don MacMonagle, macmonagle.com)

World Champion Ken Doherty performs at an exhibition game in The Gleneagle Hotel in 1997.
(© Valerie O'Sullivan)

Poker

The Ladbrokes.com Irish Poker Festival, which took place at the INEC in October 2011. Over 800 poker players from all over Europe took part in the event. (© Don MacMonagle, macmonagle.com)

Niall Smyth, winner of the top prize of €70,000 at the Ladbrokes.com Irish Poker Festival at the INEC in October 2011. (© Eamonn Keogh, macmonagle.com)

Tug of War

Irish participants battle it out at the 2006 World Indoor Tug of War Championships at the INEC. (© Valerie O'Sullivan)

Members of the English team, Diana Allcock, Rachael Knight, Gwen Simcock, Debbie Upstone and Dawn Wainwright, competing in the 2006 World Indoor Tug of War Championship at the INEC.
(© Valerie O'Sullivan)

Irish Dancing

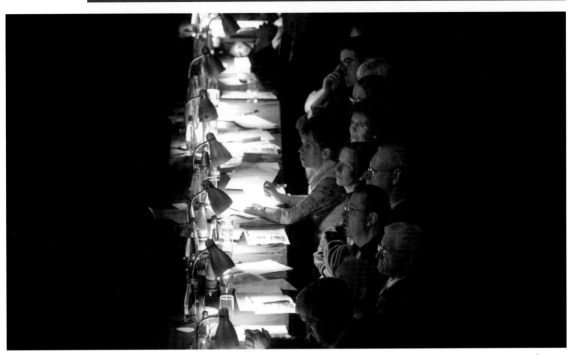

The table of judges keep a close eye on proceedings at the *Cumann Lúthchleas Gael Scór Sinsear Craobh nÉireann* at the INEC in 2005. (© Eamonn Keogh, macmonagle.com)

Adjudicator Dan Armstrong making sure all the contestants are in correct position at the *Oireachtas Rince na nÉireann* at the INEC in February 2008. (© Valerie O'Sullivan)

Dancers from Mona Rodagh, County Louth competing in the Junior Girls *Céilí* Championships at *Oireachtas Rince na hÉireann* 2010 at the INEC. (© Valerie O'Sullivan)

The 2014 *An Comhdháil* World Irish Dance Championships brought over 5,000 competitors from Ireland, America, Scotland, England and Europe to Killarney to compete for a world title. The event was officially launched at Ross Castle by dancers Sarah Silby, Ciara Silby, Vivian Moynihan, Aisling Lowe, Kayley Riordan and Emma Lowe. (© Valerie O'Sullivan)

Other Sports

Olympian rower Paul Griffin of Muckross Rowing Club trying out his new single schull in the Aquila Club pool. The boat was sponsored by Killarney businesses, The Gleneagle Hotel, Dawn Dairies and MD O'Shea's. Paul is pictured with Patrick O'Donoghue, Gleneagle Hotel and Mike Murphy, Dawn Dairies. (© Eamonn Keogh, macmonagle.com)

Dublin's Anthony Fitzgerald fighting Kirrilli Pshonko during the Pro-Boxing Tournament at the INEC in October 2008.

(© Don MacMonagle, macmonagle.com)

Former Irish International soccer player John Aldridge celebrating Ireland's win over Saudi Arabia at the INEC on 11 June 2002. (© Don MacMonagle, macmonagle.com)

Bowls Tournament at the INEC, one of the many sports catered for by The Gleneagle Hotel. (© Don MacMonagle, macmonagle.com)

Pictured at the Kerry Spring Munster Close Squash Championship, which was hosted by The Gleneagle Squash Club in February 2009, are Mike Howard (tournament director), John Cullen (Munster Squash president) and Mike Murphy (Kerry Spring Water). (© Eamonn Keogh, macmonagle.com)

The Munster Table Tennis Championships, which took place in the INEC in 2011. (© Don MacMonagle, macmonagle.com)

CHAPTER FIVE

Politics and Conferences

Life at The Gleneagle isn't always about fun. It is also a place of business where politicians, organisations and blue-chip companies gather to get work done. From political conferences to international sales meetings, The Gleneagle's unique flexibility allows it to transform from a leisure hotel into a world-class conference venue. In fact some of the world's top companies have held their conferences here – IBM, Google, Glaxo Smith Kline to name a mere few.

Politics

Paddy and Sheila O'Donoghue with An Taoiseach Jack Lynch, Mrs Lynch and Beatrice Grovenor at the State Reception for the Soroptomists, November 1972.

Mackey O'Shea receives a standing ovation from Fianna Fáil members including Charles Haughey, John O'Leary and John O'Donoghue at the Fianna Fáil convention in The Gleneagle Hotel in 1986. (© Don MacMonagle, macmonagle.com)

John O'Leary and John O'Donoghue are selected to stand as candidates for Fianna Fáil at the Convention in The Gleneagle Hotel in 1986. (© Don MacMonagle, macmonagle.com)

An Taoiseach Charles Haughey visiting Killarney for the official opening of The Aquila Club at The Gleneagle Hotel in November 1991, pictured with Sheila, Maurice and Margaret O'Donoghue and TD John O'Donoghue. (© Michelle Cooper-Galvin)

Deputy Jackie Healy Rae is hoisted by supporters at The Gleneagle Hotel after the full recount in the South Kerry constituency on 19 May 2002. A nail-biting recount was ordered when just 133 votes separated the independent candidate and Fianna Fáil's Tom Fleming. (© Don MacMonagle, macmonagle.com)

Getting down to business. Minister for Arts, Tourism and Sport John O'Donoghue pictured at Fáilte Ireland's largest travel trade fair, Meitheal in May 2003. (© Don MacMonagle, macmonagle.com)

Cecelia Ahern looks admiringly at her dad, An Taoiseach Bertie Ahern, after his keynote speech at Fianna Fáil's 69th Ard Fheis at the INEC in 2005. (© Valerie O'Sullivan)

Members of Seanad and Government
at the 69th Fianna Fáil Ard Fheis at the
INEC in October 2005. (© Valerie O'Sullivan)

Minister for Finance Brian
Lenihan addressing the
Irish League of Credit
Unions Conference at the
INEC in 2009. (© Eamonn
Keogh, macmonagle.com)

Deputy Jackie Healy Rae speaking at the Healy Rae convention in The Gleneagle Hotel in October 2010. From left to right, are: Cllr Michael Healy Rae, Cllr Danny Healy Rae and election strategist John O'Donoghue, Farranfore. Several hundred members of the Healy Rae organisation met to ratify Michael Healy Rae as a candidate in the 2012 General Election.

(© Eamonn Keogh, macmonagle.com)

Taoiseach Enda Kenny is welcomed to The Gleneagle Hotel by Patrick O'Donoghue. The Taoiseach was attending the Irish Congress of Trade Unions biennial conference in July 2011. (© Eamonn Keogh, macmonagle.com)

Minister for Education Ruairi Quinn addressing the INTO Conference at the Gleneagle Hotel in May 2012. (© Don MacMonagle, macmonagle.com)

Gerry Adams and Mary Lou McDonald pictured at the Sinn Féin Ard Fheis in the INEC in May 2012.

(© Don MacMonagle, macmonagle.com)

Party Leader Micheál Martin addressing the Fianna Fáil Ard Fheis in the INEC in March 2014.
(© Don MacMonagle, macmonagle.com)

An Tánaiste and Leader of the Labour Party Joan Burton is welcomed by Breffni Ingerton, General Manager Killarney Convention Centre ahead of the annual Labour Conference in 2015. (© Valerie O'Sullivan)

Conferences

The addition of the INEC has allowed The Gleneagle Hotel to host all sorts of national and international conferences. In 2007 the hotel welcomed the European Communities Trade Mark Association Conference. (© Don MacMonagle, macmonagle.com)

The INEC is Ireland's largest dedicated conference and events venue. Its flexible layout and design allows it to cater for conferences ranging from 25 to 2,500 delegates. It is suitable for meetings, conferences and exhibitions of all shapes and sizes, from small corporate meetings to international congresses. In 2006 it welcomed 650 delegates from 35 countries for the Association of European Hotel and Tourism Schools Conference. (© Don MacMonagle, macmonagle.com)

By night, the versatility of this
venue is truly apparent as the INEC
auditorium is transformed into a
magnificent banqueting hall.

IBM delegates enjoying
some post-conference
entertainment at the
INEC. The venue has
hosted the annual IBM
sales conference on three
separate occasions. (© Don
MacMonagle, macmonagle.com)

Delegates gather at
the INEC for Google's
EMEA Sales Conference
in October 2009. (© Don
MacMonagle, macmonagle.com)

Google CEO Eric Schmidt flew his personal Gulfstream jet into Kerry airport to address the 2,500 delegates at Google's EMEA Sales Conference in the INEC, Killarney in October 2009. (© Don MacMonagle, macmonagle.com)

Six chartered aircraft transporting over 1,000 conference delegates from across Europe, Africa and the Middle East came to land in Kerry Airport. A further 1,000 delegates travelled by chartered trains from the company's European Headquarters in Dublin. (© Don MacMonagle, macmonagle.com)

'I cannot praise the staff at the INEC, and staff in the hotels, restaurants and pubs throughout the town highly enough. Their professionalism and service levels were second to none and showcased Killarney, Kerry and Ireland to the very highest standards. The logistics of bringing 2,500 people together from all over Europe is not easy but everything worked very smoothly and we definitely showed that Ireland is among the best locations in Europe for international conferences. I would like to thank all the people of Killarney for the hospitality shown to all of us in Google.' John Herlihy, head of Google Ireland, pictured here with Patrick O'Donoghue. (© Don MacMonagle, macmonagle.com)

Killarney's biggest ever banquet. Executive Chef John Drummond and his team prepared a sumptuous meal for Google's 2,500 delegates at the INEC in October 2009. (© Don MacMonagle, macmonagle.com)

President of Ireland, Mary McAleese addressing delegates at the annual Irish Primary Principals Network Conference at the INEC in 2008. (© Valerie O'Sullivan)

Sr Stanisclaus Kennedy, Focus Ireland, pauses before she addresses the annual Irish Primary Principals Network Conference at the INEC in January 2009. (© Valerie O'Sullivan)

Irish Nurses Organisation, General Secretary Liam Doran speaking at the opening of the INO Annual Delegate Conference at the INEC. (© Eamonn Keogh, macmonagle.com)

Practicing mindfulness. Buddhist Zen Master Thich Nhat Hanh, leading a four-day residential retreat entitled 'Living Mindfully Today' at the INEC in April 2012. He was accompanied by fifty monks and nuns, and over 750 lay people. (© Valerie O'Sullivan)

Buddhist monks from Plum Village in France. From left to right: Sr Dáo Nghiém, Br Pháp Tái and Br Treasure, meditating in the seasonal blue bells in Killarney National Park as part of the 'Living Mindfully Today' retreat that took place at the INEC in April 2012. (© Valerie O'Sullivan)

CHAPTER SIX

Entertainment

From the opening of the ballroom in 1959, The Gleneagle Hotel has become synonymous with first-class entertainment and facilities. A young and enthusiastic Maurice O'Donoghue prioritised 'quality above all' and consistently booked the very best in top bands and shows, filling a huge gap in the nightlife of Killarney, and attracting punters who travelled from throughout Kerry and the adjoining counties. Since then entertainment at The Gleneagle Hotel has evolved and adapted with quality always remaining to the fore.

Cabaret was introduced to the hotel in 1965, and by 1969 it was on five nights a week throughout the summer. Audiences averaged about 500 people a night and attracted stars such as Joe Dolan, Dermot O'Brien, Johnny McEvoy, Joe Cuddy and The Furey Brothers. By 1980, the budget for the summer's entertainment had reached £100,000 with entertainment at four venues, seven nights a week. The Wolfe Tones, Brendan Grace, Christy Moore, Brendan Shine, Dickie Rock, Louise Morrissey, and Killarney's own, The Swinging Jarveys played frequently at the hotel.

The building of Ireland's National Events Centre (INEC) in 2000 greatly expanded the entertainment potential of the hotel. High-profile national and international acts, such as Cliff Richard, Blondie, Morrissey and Hozier performed in Killarney for the very first time. Today, The Gleneagle Hotel is considered one of Ireland's leading entertainment venues and hosts a wide range of events all-year-round.

1960s

Entertainers from The Gleneagle Cabaret pictured on the opening night of the summer season in 1969. Also pictured are Paddy, Sheila, Maurice and Maura O'Donoghue. (© Donal MacMonagle, macmonagle.com)

Owen Neville serenades his audience in the ballroom in June 1969. (© Kevin Coleman)

A quiet corner of the sun lounge at the GlenEagle Hotel.

Big Name Bands Booked For GlenEagle Dancing

FROM PAGE 6

too often they are small, poky little places, with queer mottled mirrors and chipped hand basins where it is impossible to wash your hands in comfort, or to comb your hair because of the crush. "Before the extension the other ladies' room was much too small and crowded," he said as he led me along to the cafeteria which is to have a face-lift to blend in with the rest of the decorations. "We are putting a gents' room at the end and this also will be enlarged," he added.

The cloakrooms have been designed to cater for many hundreds of coats with the minimum delay. Dancers at the end of the evening will leave by special doors leading out of the cloakrooms and again these doors have been built in order to clear the hall of people in a very short time.

'a great help'

Leaving the hall, we made our way out to the car park which is another feature of the GlenEagle. "Watching the crowds coming and going over the years I know what they want and I have to designed the car park that there are no jams or hold-ups. Each car parks at an angle leaving space for the other to get clear and away without delay." Last year the car park was capable of taking some 400 cars but Mr. O'Donoghue has again enlarged and the parking lot will now comfortably accommodate 600 cars. "We have two entrances to the park, which is a great help," added Mr. O'Donoghue.

When I asked Mr. O'Donoghue why he had gone to so much expense to alter what was already an attractive dancing centre he informed me that he believed in moving with the times. "We were finding that the ballroom was not large enough to accommodate the large number of dancers. The answer to the problem was to extend and that is what we have done. As well as this, we found it would be wiser to have a separate entrance to the hall-room and as well as enlarging the GlenEagle we have also provided a new and independent entrance. Work began last September and now you are looking at the finished results. If the need arises again I will extend even further," he added.

As well as being an ideal dancing centre capable of accommodating several thousand dancers, the new ballroom is also geared to take international conferences, outings, socials, school trips, coach parties and day trippers. Last year alone, before it was extended, the ballroom catered for some three or four thousand students on college outings. Talking about this, Mr. O'Donoghue said that really it was difficult to cater for them in the hotel proper, but now they had the cafeteria and the snack bar completely independent of the hotel.

"We have the car park for coaches . . . no matter how big they build there," he said.

"We can take any size conference in the ballroom and then in inclement weather outings can happily be catered for in bright surroundings with all comforts," Mr. O'Donoghue continued.

ample room

He told me that it was their intention to cater extensively for touring parties as well as for socials and weddings. "For a small social we block off part of the ballroom in order to provide the cosy atmosphere of smaller functions and then we have the space for large, ambitious affairs."

I learned that the ballroom provides good steady employment for

local people, having a staff of sixteen. These include cloak-room and car park attendants, doormen, ticket sellers and snack bar and cafeteria employees.

Big name Irish and Cross Channel bands have been booked and no doubt "Royal" fans will be delighted to hear that the Royal Showband will be visiting the GlenEagle in the near future.

While the ballroom opens officially on Easter Sunday night, the hall has already had an 'airing.' Dance lovers flocked there on St. Patrick's night and although packed to capacity, the fans still had ample room for dancing and 'sitting it out.' From that night some idea of how the hall would stand up to large attendances and what slight alterations would be required to make it truly Killarney's number one ballroom was gained. It was on that night also that the decision was made by Mr. O'Donoghue to extend the parking lot even further and an extra laneway is at present being laid out. This will be banked by a small lawn and flowers with steps set in at various points for easy access to the hall.

Leaving the ballroom behind, Mr. O'Donoghue led me back into the hotel to show me ten new bedrooms (all with their own bathrooms) which he had added last year. For this extension Mr. O'Donoghue went 'up,' adding another floor and a flight of stairs.

last word

On our way, he told me that as a result of the extension to the ballroom it had been possible for him to add an additional four single bedrooms to another part of the hotel. "These will be ideal for over-night parties," he commented leading the way up the richly carpeted stairway.

Like the rest of this hotel, the new bedrooms are the last word in comfort and taste. Pastel pinks, sunshine yellows, dove-greys and eggshell blues have been used on walls with matching bed-spreads and curtains and wall to wall carpeting for the floor. As well as space for suit-cases, built in ward-

---

Cooking herrings the French way

FRANCE has long been famous for excellent cuisine. Visitors from all over the world rave about the wonderful food there. What is the secret? Imagination and variety. One of the striking features in French cooking is the excellence of the fish dishes, and many of the most interesting of these are made from cheaper fish. So you can eat in style and still balance your budget. Why not try herrings as they eat them in Calais, the famous French fishing port?

HERRING CALAISIENNE

Ingredients: 4 fresh herrings; 2 hard boiled eggs; 1 slice of white bread; 1 dessertspoon of chopped herbs; 1 small onion; 2 cloves garlic; salt and pepper; 2 tomatoes; 1 tablespoon of tomato puree; peppercorns; 1 pint stock; 2½ ozs. butter; ½ oz. flour; 1 bay leaf.

METHOD

Herrings: Remove heads. Split down backs with a sharp knife to remove bone. Wash and dry well, and fill with the following stuffing: Shell and finely chop eggs, put into bowl with chopped up herring roes, finely chopped garlic, half chopped onion, the herbs, salt and pepper, and lastly bind the stuffing with slice of bread which has been soaked with 1 pint of stock. When the herrings are neatly filled with the stuffing, place in a fire-proof dish and pour over a little melted butter and cover with a piece of buttered paper. Cook in a moderate oven for 25 minutes. Remove and keep warm.

SAUCE

Melt 1 oz. of butter in a pan, add sliced onion and a few peppercorns, bay leaf, tomatoes and tomato puree, cover and leave to cook slowly for ten minutes. Remove, stir in flour, add a little salt and pour in ½ pint of stock, stir over the fire until it comes to the boil. Push through a strainer, return to pan and stir in 1 oz. of butter.

SERVING

Pour on sauce on bottom of dish. Arrange the herrings on the top. Garnish round the dish with the slices of lemon and serve. Approximate time: ¾ hour.

Modernisation of Killarney Abbatoir

THE modernisation of Killarney Abbatoir was discussed at this week's meeting of Killarney Urban Council, when a report was read from the Town Surveyor, Mr. T. O'Sullivan, B.E., with recommendations proposed to him by Mr. Owen Gleeson, Veterinary Surgeon.

Mr. Gleeson suggested the installation of electrically worked pulleys and a pit with a ramp for the disposal of offal. The Town Surveyor estimated that the proposed renovations would cost £176.

Mr. M. Moynihan said that the butchers held that the facilities at the abattoir were very inadequate. He thought the Co. Manager should consider the whole matter in order to bring the abattoir in line with modern requirements.

Mr. D. Doona said there was no supply of hot water in the abattoir, which was very necessary, and this was not mentioned by the surveyor.

On the suggestion of the chairman, Mr. T. P. Clifford, the County Manager is to inspect the facilities at the newly designed abattoir in Tralee and report back to the Council for the estimates meeting, when the matter will again be discussed.

Schoolboy Footballers Congratulated

ON the proposition of Mr. M. O'Leary, Killarney Urban Council extended congratulations to St. Brendan's Seminary on winning Corn Mumhan this year in the Munster Colleges senior football championship.

eye-catching

In the spacious but cosy bar, he went on to tell me something of his plans for the gardens in the hotel which he expected to get around to in the very near future. He plans to have wide expanses of green lawns, banks of flowers and white seating. This will be just another additional amenity for hotel guests and it will certainly look very eye-catching from the road.

On such occasions, conversation tends to drift, and it wasn't long before I was held enthralled listening to Mr. O'Donoghue discuss Irish folklore and explain some of the meanings of place names in and around Killarney and further afield.

I learned he had a fund of knowledge on such matters and that busy as he is with his chemist shop in town he still finds time to delve into the past of Ireland. His love of old things is very apparent and so also is his interest in Ireland of old.

Like many people, he feels it is a great pity that some of Killarney's old time happenings are not revived pointing out that this would prove an added attraction for tourists.

"I recall that long before the Festival of Kerry was launched people were coming here and clamouring to hear the 'Rose of Tralee' being sung. I thought it was a mistake not to do something about it. However Tralee has and Killarney should now also look around for some Festival or other which is part and parcel of Killarney," he said.

planning ahead

It was dinner time before I began to take my leave and I certainly had a lot of food for thought. In a few hours I'd seen a modern up-to-date hotel that had 'grown' as it were from the very earth . . . a ballroom which is before its time but exactly what 1963 dancers want . . . and a car park which is geared to house hundreds of cars, without any traffic jams.

Mr. O'Donoghue wisely realises what people want and as far as possible he is aiming to provide them with it.

While I was being shown alterations and extensions I'm sure that Mr. O'Donoghue was looking over my shoulder into future years and planning ahead. Perhaps a more I was admiring he was planning to remove. I don't know, but I certainly got the feeling that he is moving way ahead all the time.

I had meant to ask Mr. O'Donoghue how the hotel got its name, but ended each speed and action I forgot. However, I'm sure I'll visit there again, as most people feel they have to do having visited the GlenEagle once.

1970s

Pictured are the legendary Joe Loss & his Orchestra on their visit to the Gleneagle in the early '70's ....

The legendary Joe Loss and his Orchestra on their visit to The Gleneagle in the early 1970s.

The original Swinging Jarveys pictured outside The Gleneagle Hotel in 1975. (© Donal MacMonagle, macmonagle.com)

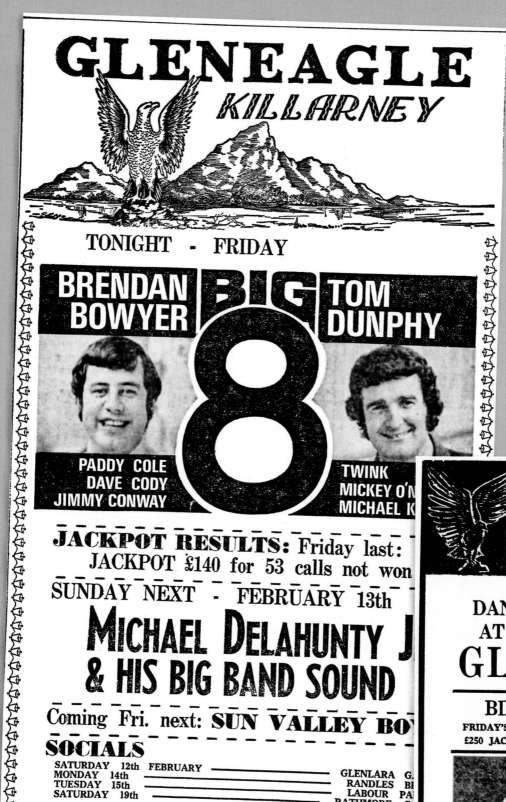

The Showband Era in full swing! (© *The Kerryman*)

GLENEAGLE
KILLARNEY

★ Easter Week-end Attractions ★

SATURDAY - Fantastic Double Bill
IN CABARET

RONNIE DREW
LUKE KELLY
AND THE
DUBLINERS
FOLLOWED BY DANCING TO
TOMMY DRENNAN &
THE TOP LEAGUE
CABARET 9.30—11 approx. DANCING UNTIL 1 a.m. Cover Charge 50p
FULLY LICENSED

EASTER SUNDAY
DICKIE ROC &
THE MIAMI

MONDAY - Candlelight Dance with
MICK DELAHUNTY
FULLY LICENSED

GLE Hotel
Country Club.
KILLARNEY

NIGHT, FRIDAY:
st of Pop and Country from
CK RUANE
SUNDAY NEXT:
The Queen of Country
EILEEN KING
WITH THE
**COUNTRY
FLAVOUR**
NG, FRIDAY NEXT:
MARGO
AND THE
NTRY FOLK
URDAY NIGHT
RET/DANCING:
fe Tones
NG TILL 1 a.m. WITH
HE CINDERS
on stage at 9.30 sharp. "Be early."
enEagle Country Club now.

Dancing the night away to the Swinging Jarveys in the ballroom of The Gleneagle Hotel. (© Don MacMonagle, macmonagle.com)

The Swinging Jarveys – one of The Gleneagle Hotel's resident bands.

1980s

The launch of the 1980 Gleneagle Summer Cabaret.

Gay Byrne's Concert Tour visited
The Gleneagle in June 1980.

John McNally, resident singer with the Swinging Jarveys, takes to the stage for The Gleneagle Cabaret in 1982. (© Don MacMonagle, macmonagle.com)

Promotional poster for the 1982 Gleneagle Summer Cabaret.

Promotional poster for
the 1986 Gleneagle
Summer Cabaret.

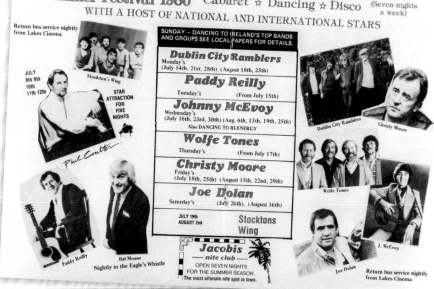

Country music star Dermot Moriarty and friends at The Gleneagle Cabaret in 1986. (© Don MacMonagle,
macmonagle.com)

1986 poster for late-night dancing at Jacobis nite club at The Gleneagle Hotel.

Summer brochure 1987.

The Kerryman, 29 July 1988.

Poster for Phil Coulter concert.

Poster for the 1989 Gleneagle Summer Cabaret.

There's no show like a Joe show. Joe Dolan performs at his regular Saturday night show in the ballroom of the hotel as part of the legendary Gleneagle Summer Cabaret.

(© Don MacMonagle, macmonagle.com)

1990s

My Heart is in Ireland. Brian Warfield of The Wolfe Tones performing in the ballroom of The Gleneagle Hotel. (© Eamonn Keogh, macmonagle.com)

The Furey Brothers and Davy Arthur pictured in the ballroom as part of the legendary annual Summer Cabaret. (© Don MacMonagle, macmonagle.com)

Special Guest ★ Appearances ★

MONDAYS
Traditional Irish Cabaret
Kerry Slides, Jigs, Reels, Songs and Stories.

TUESDAYS ★
Brendan Grace
Hilarious family entertainment
with Ireland's Top Comedian.

WEDNESDAYS ★
Johnny McEvoy
with Special Guests ★
Ireland's most versatile Ballad
Singer plays a wide selection of
traditional and international favourites.

THURSDAYS ★
The Wolfe Tones
Make the rafters roar with a good
old-fashioned ballad session from
Ireland's leading Traditional Group.

FRIDAYS ★
Traditional Irish Cabaret
Kerry Slides, Jigs, Reels, Songs and Stories.
Followed by: Top Dance/Cabaret Acts

SATURDAYS
Joe Dolan ★
Classic Golden and Modern hits from
Ireland's No. 1 Dance and Cabaret Artiste.

SUNDAYS ★
Red Hurley
National TV/Cabaret Star performs
a wide range of material from his
extensive repertoire.

The Dixies ★
(Aug 22 & 29) Dance & swing with this legendary Cork Band

ALL SHOWS FOLLOWED BY EURODISCO

BAR MUSIC EVERY NIGHT - NO COVER CHARGE

Summer entertainment
festival guide 1993.

Leading the way in new and
emerging music,
The Prodigy performed at
The Gleneagle in 1993.

Wild Noise Promotions in Association with
X.L. Records & JVC Presents

THE PRODIGY

THE GLENEAGLE HOTEL
KILLARNEY
•FRIDAY 27TH AUGUST 1993•

£10.50

1347

Management accept no responsibility for damage to persons or property
No ticket No entry • All Prodigy tickets & bus tickets must be purchased
before August 7th

Joe Dolan in full flight as he celebrates the millennium at his concert on New Year's Eve
1999 in the ballroom of The Gleneagle Hotel. (© Don MacMonagle, macmonagle.com)

Local children from the Tara Little Drama School, Kerry, performing in the West End production of *Annie* at the INEC in August 2007. (© Valerie O'Sullivan)

Curtain call. The Coronas perform at the INEC in December 2012.

(© Valerie O'Sullivan)

The Coronas live on stage at the INEC in December 2012. (© Valerie O'Sullivan)

Trad supergroup Altan at the INEC in November 2006. (© Valerie O'Sullivan)

The cast of Disney's *Beauty and The Beast* visit Muckross House ahead of their performance at the INEC in November 2008. (© Valerie O'Sullivan)

Bryan Adams
performing at the
INEC in January 2010.

(© Valerie O'Sullivan)

Fans flock to the INEC to see Bell X1 performing in November 2006. (© Valerie O'Sullivan)

Big Country, the popular Scottish band pictured playing in the INEC in July 2011. (© Valerie O'Sullivan)

Debbie Harry, aka 'Blondie', performing at the INEC Killarney in July 2004. (© Valerie O'Sullivan)

The cast of *Bohemian Rhapsody – The Musical* performing in the world premiere of the show at the INEC in June 2012. (© Valerie O'Sullivan)

Chris De Burgh plays to
a packed audience at the
INEC in August 2005.

(© Valerie O'Sullivan)

Boys II Men performing at the INEC in May 2010. (© Valerie O'Sullivan)

Killarney native and rising star Jessie Buckley, with Finbarr Coffey and Gerry Adams, performing in *Carousel* by Killarney Musical Society at the INEC in March 2008. (© Valerie O'Sullivan)

Shaolin monks performing their martial arts as part of the Chinese State Circus acrobatic performance in the INEC in April 2013. (© Valerie O'Sullivan)

Sailing away with David Gray at the INEC in December 2014. (© Valerie O'Sullivan)

The legendary Christy Moore in concert at the INEC in April 2008.

(© Valerie O'Sullivan)

Maire Brennan, lead singer
with Clannad, giving a
haunting performance at
the INEC in May 2008.
(© Valerie O'Sullivan)

Des Bishop in full flight at the INEC in July 2008. (© Valerie O'Sullivan)

Don McLean in concert at
the INEC in August 2005.

(© Valerie O'Sullivan)

The West End hit musical *Fiddler on the Roof* at the INEC in August 2008. (© Valerie O'Sullivan)

A scene from the opening night of the West End production *Footloose* at the INEC in October 2008. (© Valerie O'Sullivan)

Comedian Dara Ó Briain performing at the INEC in February 2010. (© Valerie O'Sullivan)

Frames frontman
Glen Hansard
playing to delighted
fans at the INEC.
(© Valerie O'Sullivan)

The Gipsy Kings live at the INEC in 2006. (© Valerie O'Sullivan)

Mary Black performing in the 'Help for Haiti' concert at the INEC in February 2010. (© Valerie O'Sullivan)

Garry Moore performing at the 'Help for Haiti' concert at the INEC in February 2010. (© Valerie O'Sullivan)

Disney's *High School Musical* at the INEC in January 2009. (© Valerie O'Sullivan)

Hozier performing live at the INEC in December 2014. (© Valerie O'Sullivan)

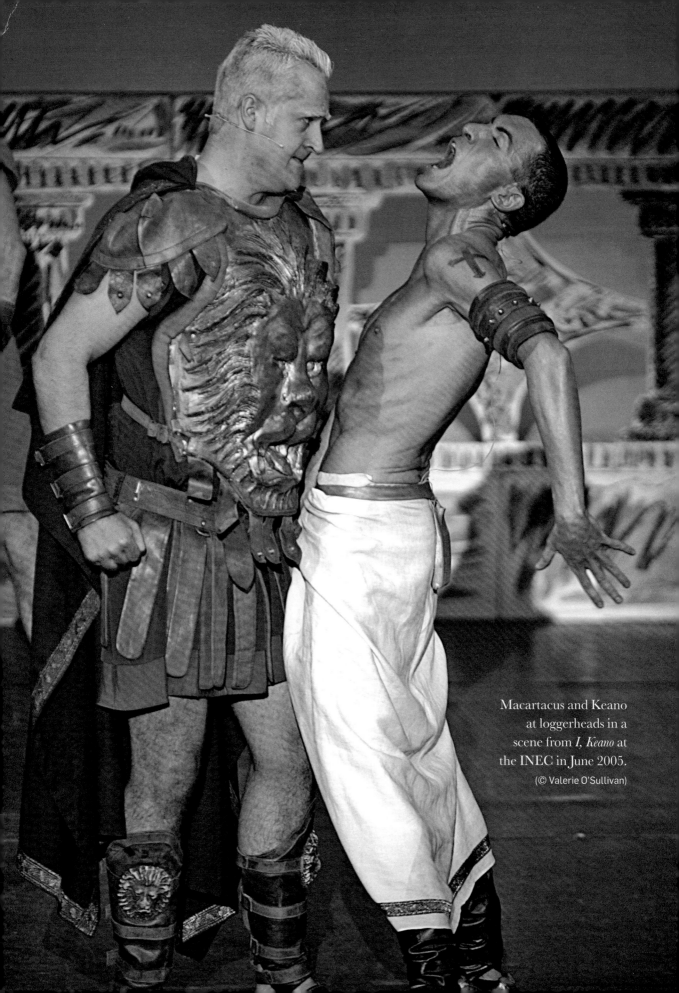

Macartacus and Keano
at loggerheads in a
scene from *I, Keano* at
the INEC in June 2005.

(© Valerie O'Sullivan)

Singer-songwriter James Morrison in concert at the INEC in August 2012. (© Valerie O'Sullivan)

Jedward perform yet another sell-out concert in the INEC in August 2011. (© Valerie O'Sullivan)

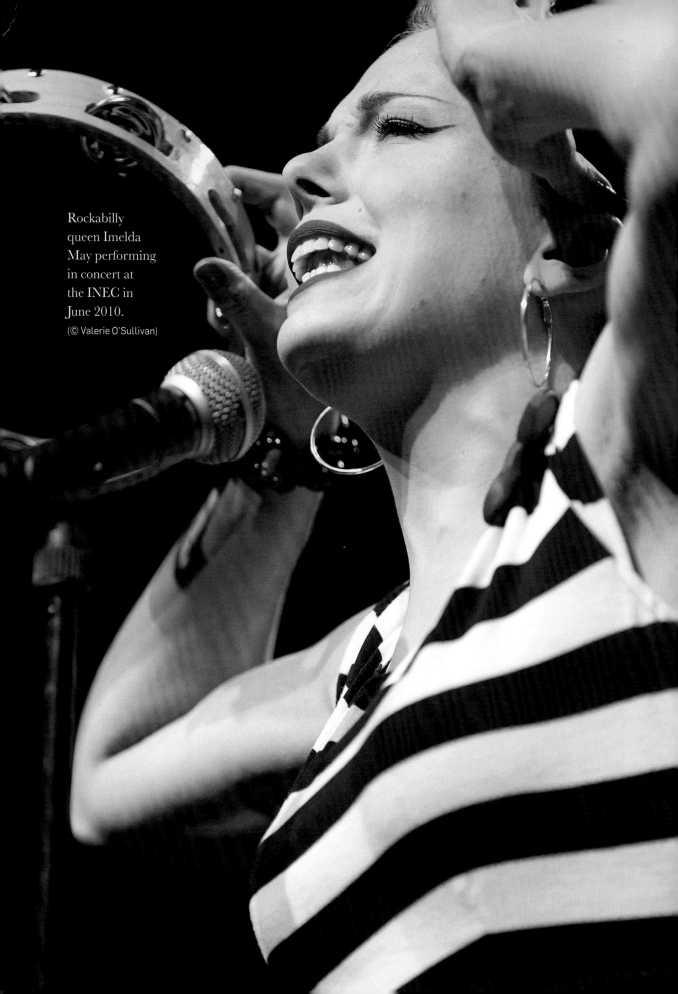

Rockabilly
queen Imelda
May performing
in concert at
the INEC in
June 2010.
(© Valerie O'Sullivan)

Fans of the late Joe Dolan flock to Killarney for the Joe Dolan tribute weekend. Huge crowds gathered to watch Joe on screen, while his band played live over three nights in July 2008. (© Valerie O'Sullivan)

Spanish tenor José Carreras performing at the INEC Killarney in July 2004. (© Valerie O'Sullivan)

Legendary singer-songwriter Kenny Rogers performing at the INEC in July 2013. (© Valerie O'Sullivan)

Irish rock band Kodaline perform to huge crowds at the INEC in March 2014. (© Valerie O'Sullivan)

Argentinean tenor
José Cura performing
at the INEC in
November 2005.
(© Valerie O'Sullivan)

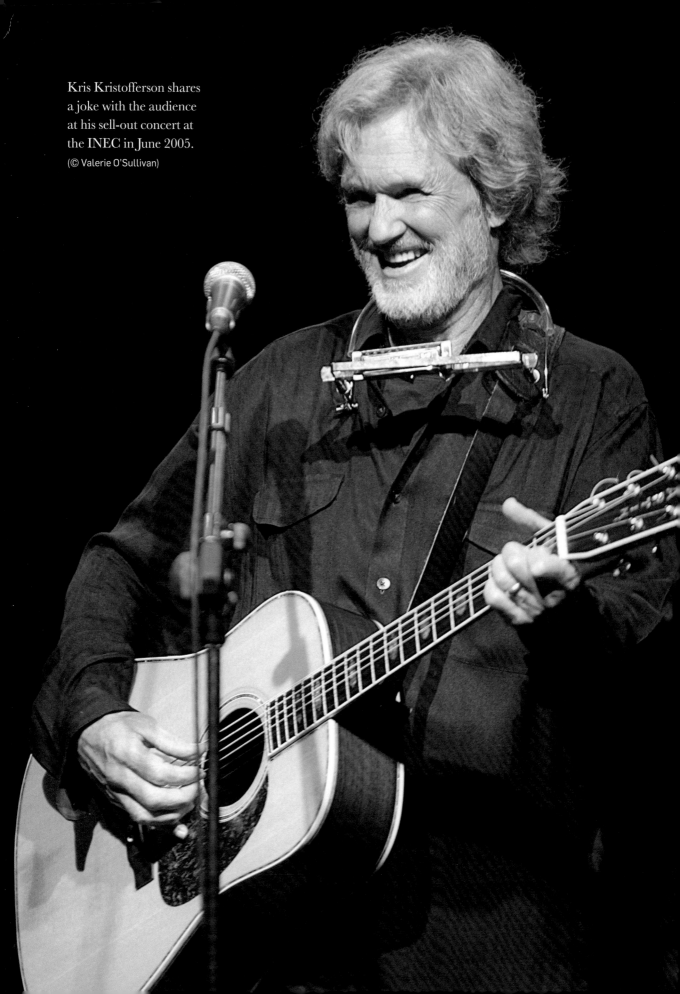

Kris Kristofferson shares a joke with the audience at his sell-out concert at the INEC in June 2005.
(© Valerie O'Sullivan)

A scene from Puccini's *La Bohème* performed by Opus1 Opera at the INEC in March 2006. (© Valerie O'Sullivan)

A scene from *Le Grand Cirque*, which featured an international cast of world-class acrobats and performers. *Le Grand Cirque* visited the INEC in August 2008. (© Valerie O'Sullivan)

David McCabe and fellow dancers at the Kerry premiere of Michael Flatley's *Lord of the Dance* at the INEC in July 2012. (© Valerie O'Sullivan)

Morrissey performing in concert at the INEC in April 2006. (© Valerie O'Sullivan)

Scottish singer-
songwriter KT Tunstall
performing at the INEC
in December 2005.
(© Valerie O'Sullivan)

Nathan Carter rings in the New Year at his sold-out concert at the INEC in December 2014. (© Valerie O'Sullivan)

Country-singing sensation Nathan Carter, who filled the INEC three nights in a row in May 2014.

(© Valerie O'Sullivan)

Nathan Carter's fans sing along at the country-music star's sold-out concert at the INEC on New Year's Eve 2014. (© Valerie O'Sullivan)

Shane McGowan celebrates the New Year with his legendary song *Fairytale of New York* at a concert at the INEC in December 2008. (© Valerie O'Sullivan)

A scene from The Killarney Musical Society's production of *Oliver* at the INEC in March 2009.
(© Valerie O'Sullivan)

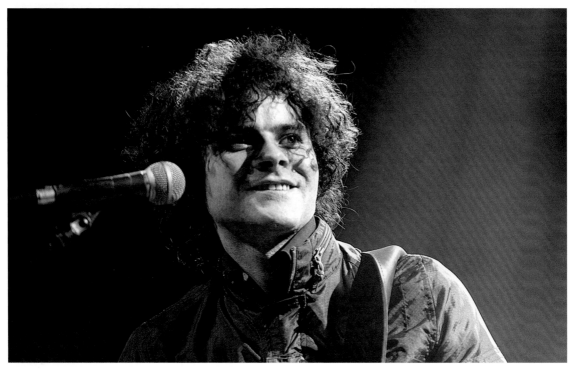

Saints and sinners. Paddy Casey performing to over 3,000 adoring fans at the INEC in December 2004.
(© Valerie O'Sullivan)

Paul Brady playing at the INEC in May 2005. (© Valerie O'Sullivan)

Paolo Nutini performing
to a packed audience at the
INEC in September 2010.

(© Valerie O'Sullivan)

INEC golden girl Sharon
Shannon performing
with her band on
New Year's Eve 2013.
(© Valerie O'Sullivan)

Revving up! Irish band the Revs soundcheck before their gig at the INEC in December 2005. (© Valerie O'Sullivan)

American country and western sensations Rascal Flatts in concert at the INEC in July 2013. (© Valerie O'Sullivan)

French pianist Richard Clayderman in concert at the INEC in April 2013. (© Valerie O'Sullivan)

Westlife star Shane Filan brings his solo tour to the INEC in December 2014. (© Valerie O'Sullivan)

Irish dance phenomenon *Riverdance* takes to the stage at the INEC in September 2006. (© Valerie O'Sullivan)

Killarney Musical Society
performing *The Wiz* at
the INEC in March 2010.
(© Valerie O'Sullivan)

A scene from John B. Keane's *Sive*, performed by the Druid Theatre
Company at the INEC in April 2003. (© Valerie O'Sullivan)

Soulful Sinead O'Connor
in concert at the INEC
in October 2002.

(© Valerie O'Sullivan)

Snow Patrol Reworked at the INEC in December 2009. Sixteen extra musicians join the acclaimed band on stage to celebrate their successful career. (© Valerie O'Sullivan)

Stereophonics in concert at the INEC in November 2007. (© Valerie O'Sullivan)

Mike Scott of
The Waterboys
performing at the
INEC in August 2004.
(© Valerie O'Sullivan)

Brian Dennehy plays
Bull McCabe in John
B. Keane's *The Field* at the
INEC in February 2011.
(© Valerie O'Sullivan)

A scene from John B. Keane's *The Field* starring Brian Dennehy at the INEC in February 2011. (© Valerie O'Sullivan)

The Frames ring in 2006 with a full house at the INEC. (© Valerie O'Sullivan)

Regular INEC performers The High Kings pictured live on stage. (© Valerie O'Sullivan)

Mick Lally performing in John B. Keane's *The Matchmaker* at the INEC in October 2006. (© Valerie O'Sullivan)

Danny O'Donoghue, lead singer with The Script, performing at the INEC in September 2009.
(© Valerie O'Sullivan)

Tommy Fleming performing to a capacity audience at the INEC in January 2006. (© Valerie O'Sullivan)

A night at the opera.
Opus 1 Opera perform
Giacomo Puccini's *Tosca* at
the INEC in March 2006.
(© Valerie O'Sullivan)

UB40 performing to a packed audience
at the INEC in November 2007.
(© Valerie O'Sullivan)

Van Morrison performing
in concert at the
INEC in April 2006.
(© Valerie O'Sullivan)

Kerry natives Walking on Cars play to packed home crowd at the INEC in December 2014. (© Valerie O'Sullivan)

Sir Bob Geldof pictured on stage at the INEC in November 2001. (© Don MacMonagle, macmonagle.com)

One of the most famous guitars in the world, owned and played by legendary country and western singer Willie Nelson, at the INEC in June 2010. The artist still prefers his old guitar, battered and bruised after fifty years of play, to a new one. (© Don MacMonagle, macmonagle.com)

The Dubliners perform for RTÉ's *Coulter & Company*, a nine-part series filmed in the INEC throughout the summer of 2005. (© Eamonn Keogh, macmonagle.com)

INEC regular Daniel O'Donnell receiving the 'Chairde Chill Airne' Order of Inisfallen Award in recognition of his outstanding contribution to Killarney's economic development over many years. The award was presented by Mayor of Killarney John Joe Culloty and president of Killarney Chamber of Tourism and Commerce Johnny McGuire in the INEC in August 2014. (© Don MacMonagle, macmonagle.com)

Performers participating in the Teen Spirit Show at the INEC in March 2012. Through music, Teen Spirit celebrates the talents and Christian faith of teenagers from all over Kerry. (© Eamon Keogh, macmonagle.com)